Business Continuity Management System

Business Continuity Management System

A Complete Guide to
Implementing ISO 22301

Wei Ning Zechariah Wong
Jianping Shi

KoganPage

LONDON PHILADELPHIA NEW DELHI

Publisher's note

Every possible effort has been made to ensure that the information contained in this book is accurate at the time of going to press, and the publishers and authors cannot accept responsibility for any errors or omissions, however caused. No responsibility for loss or damage occasioned to any person acting, or refraining from action, as a result of the material in this publication can be accepted by the editor, the publisher or any of the authors.

First published in Great Britain and the United States in 2015 by Kogan Page Limited

2nd Floor, 45 Gee Street	1518 Walnut Street, Suite 1100	4737/23 Ansari Road
London EC1V 3RS	Philadelphia PA 19102	Daryaganj
United Kingdom	USA	New Delhi 110002
www.koganpage.com		India

© Wei Ning Zechariah Wong and Jianping Shi, 2015

The right of Wei Ning Zechariah Wong and Jianping Shi to be identified as the authors of this work has been asserted by them in accordance with the Copyright, Designs and Patents Act 1988.

ISBN   978 0 7494 6911 5
E-ISBN   978 0 7494 6912 2

British Library Cataloguing-in-Publication Data

A CIP record for this book is available from the British Library.

Library of Congress Cataloging-in-Publication Data

Wong, Wei Ning Zechariah.
    Business continuity management system : a complete guide to implementing iso 22301 / Wei Ning Zechariah Wong, Jianping Shi.
        pages cm
        ISBN 978-0-7494-6911-5 (paperback) – ISBN 978-0-7494-6912-2 (ebk)   1. Crisis management. 2. Emergency management–Planning.   3. Data protection.   4. Computer networks–Security measures.   I. Shi, Jianping.   II. Title.
    HD49.W667 2014
    658.4'70218--dc23
                                                                                                2014027017

Typeset by Amnet
Print production managed by Jellyfish
Printed and bound in Great Britain by Ashford Colour Press Ltd

In memory of my beloved father
— JS

CONTENTS

ABBREVIATIONS

Best practice organization (BPO)
Business-as-usual (BAU)
Business Continuity Institute (BCI)
Business continuity management (BCM)
Business continuity management system (BCMS)
Business continuity plan (BCP)
Business continuity resource requirements analysis (BCRRA)
Business impact analysis (BIA)
Continuous professional development (CPD)
Crisis management plan (CMP)
Critical success factor (CSF)
Disaster Recovery Institute International (DRII)
Enterprise risk management (ERM)
Function restoration plan (FSP)
Incident command centre (ICC)
Incident management plan (IMP)
Incident management structure (IMS)
Information security (IS)
Information technology disaster recovery (ITDR)
Key performance indicator (KPI)
Level of business continuity (LBC)
Management of business continuity (MBC)
Maximum tolerable period of disruption (MTPD)
Plan-Do-Check-Act (PDCA)
Political, economic, social and technological (PEST)
Process recovery plan (PRP)
Recovery point objective (RPO)
Recovery time objective (RTO)
Responsible, accountable, consulted and informed (RACI)
Risk assessment (RA)

Specific, measurable, achievable, realistic and time-bound (SMART)
Statement of applicability (SoA)
Strengths, weaknesses, opportunities and threats (SWOT)
Training needs analysis (TNA)
Uninterrupted power system (UPS)

LIST OF TABLES

LIST OF FIGURES

Introduction

Business continuity management (BCM) continues to grow in terms of the importance and value to organizational activities. This is evident by the publication of the International Standard for BCM: ISO 22301 (Societal Security – Business Continuity Management Systems – Requirements), which demonstrates the recognition of the subject in enabling corporate success and optimizing service availability. In addition, today's BCM population is made up of new entrants in the fields of management consulting, information assurance, risk and insurance, compliance and quality, and, surprisingly, arts and history, which will definitely bring a kaleidoscope of novel thoughts to the profession. This diversity perhaps can be viewed as an indicator of a popular discipline in the 21st century.

Since its publication in 2012, ISO 22301 has been the touchstone in the development and management of an effective business continuity management system (BCMS). Though the requirements are accompanied by the guidance, ISO 22313, which provides useful explanation of the principles of the requirements, it does not provide *all* the necessary information on 'how' the key processes are established. Following the advent of the International Standard, many books have attempted to provide guidance on the implementation of the BCMS. However, most literature are either brief in content or do not provide the pertinent details to the readers. There still exists a deficiency of a handbook that addresses the whole lifecycle of the BCMS.

This book endeavours to address that gap, by providing in detail real case examples and approaches based on the authors' experiences. It is intended to be helpful to both new and seasoned business continuity practitioners who are responsible for the BCMS in their organizations. It describes the underlying concepts of the key activities of the BCMS and how each stage of the management system relates to one another. It explains the different issues that must be addressed at all stages throughout the lifecycle of the BCMS. A broad range of connected issues are introduced to enable business continuity practitioners to enhance their knowledge as well as to address the organizational challenges. A key strength of this book is that it provides proven techniques and suggests how they may be adapted to meet the individual's requirements and context. In particular, it proposes easy-to-use assessment methodologies to evaluate the organization's BCMS performance (Chapter 8) and explains how an effective BCMS control system is established (Chapter 9).

This book is structured based on ISO 22301. It comprises 10 chapters. Chapter 1 provides the readers the perspective of business continuity in the corporate setting. It presents an overview of the BCM lifecycle, which allows seasoned practitioners to revisit the key processes and introduces new entrants to the subject. Chapter 2 concentrates on the principles of the BCMS and its underlying approach – Plan-Do-Check-Act (PDCA). The chapter offers a review into the essential components of the BCMS. This would be particularly useful for organizations that are seeking to develop a systemic and effective BCM. Chapters 3 to 9 encapsulate the seven main clauses of ISO 22301, namely, Context of the Organization, Leadership, Planning, Support, Operation, Performance Evaluation and Improvement; they collectively form the all-encompassing approach of planning, implementing, managing and continually improving the BCMS. The final chapter, Chapter 10, identifies the organizational barriers that can hamper the effective implementation of the BCMS and offers a series of strategies to overcome those management challenges.

A unique feature of this book is that it offers the readers the choice of reading the book in its entirety (for those wishing to understand the planning and establishment of a BCMS), whilst also allowing them to choose particular components of the BCMS – a quick overview of the chapter is provided to enable them to pick the topics that are of greatest interest to them. In addition, a checklist is included at the end of each chapter to highlight the key activities or items that should be in place in order to establish an effective BCMS.

It is the authors' hope that the readers of this book can take away what is most relevant to them; the intention is to complement their own experiences so that they can derive appropriate solutions. It is particularly aimed at equipping business continuity practitioners with the knowledge, skills and ammunition to position BCM into a value-added activity of strategic importance within their organizations. This would have achieved our objective. As such, a lengthy introduction would not be necessary. Business continuity in the 21st century is here to stay. This book is intended to act as a catalyst to accelerate progress on the journey from business continuity management to business continuity management *system*, both by enhancing the BCM competence of the individual readers and by contributing to the development of a shared knowledge for implementing ISO 22301 in organizations.

Fundamentals of business continuity management

01

> **OVERVIEW**
>
> - This chapter provides the official definition of business continuity management (BCM) and outlines its distinctive characteristics.
> - It underlines the principles and functions of BCM in the corporate setting.
> - It goes on to highlight the application of BCM in the organization – ranging from strategic to operational activities.
> - Finally, the chapter describes the BCM programme lifecycle and processes generally adopted in the industry.

Background

Business evolves in rapidly changing environments, often driven by the pace of technological advancements, new regulations, increased competition and demanding customers. These drivers have fundamentally shaped organizations' emphasis on objectives based on time, quality and compliance. Some of these could present opportunities to organizations, whilst others could seriously damage their performance if they are inadequately managed.

Business continuity management (BCM) is a proactive approach that can maximize business opportunities. It enables organizations to optimize the continuity of operations, thereby safeguarding their corporate performance. It is a versatile discipline that encapsulates the multidisciplinary characteristics of management and technical subjects. The discipline is about the management of threats and their impacts to critical operations. Predominantly, it improves the organization's capacity to withstand the impact of an incident that may otherwise jeopardize its ability to achieve its objectives.

Being a corporate initiative, BCM should be driven from executive management. At board level, BCM is a planning tool that helps senior management make business decisions. The growing understanding of the need to safeguard interests of key stakeholders along with awareness of BCM in corporate governance has eased its introduction. Nonetheless, it should become an integral part of the organization's strategic and day-to-day management practice in order to establish a lasting culture of resilience.

What is business continuity management?

The most widely accepted definition of business continuity management (BCM) is a holistic management process that identifies potential threats to an organization and the impacts to business operations those threats, if realized, might cause, and which provides a framework for building organizational resilience with the capability of an effective response that safeguards the interests of its key stakeholders, reputation, brand and value-creating activities.

This definition forms the official definition of ISO 22301, the Disaster Recovery Institute (DRI) International and the Business Continuity Institute (BCI). It is developed by leading experts in the BCM industry and reflects the very nature of the discipline works in organizations.

One distinctive characteristic of BCM is that it adopts a wide range of methodologies from other branches of management subjects, notably, risk, strategy, finance and project management. This denotes an all-encompassing management approach of establishing a corporate capability of safeguarding the organization's high-value assets.

This management discipline is broadly made up of two interrelating activities: analytical and planning. The analytical activity is an in-depth examination into the corporate functions, operations and business drivers that contribute to the organization's business performance. It is supported by a series of methodologies that assess threats and their impacts to critical operations. On the other hand, the planning activity develops the organization's business continuity capability in response to an incident. It comprises key processes with defined outputs that address the business continuity requirements identified in the analytical activity.

The principles of business continuity management

One of the primary functions of BCM is to protect the organization by maintaining business performance, whilst at the same time minimizing the negative impacts during an incident. In order to achieve an effective implementation of BCM in the organization, it is worth noting its basic concepts:

- Long-range focus
- Leadership
- Governance
- Good business practice
- Multidisciplinary function
- Communication
- Value preservation
- Adaptation

Long-range focus

BCM is a strategic initiative that can influence corporate performance. The BCM programme can enable the organization to generate competitive advantage through enhanced operational resilience. Its activities can be incorporated into the strategic planning process to identify threats that have potentially significant implications to an organization.

When making critical decisions, the BCM methodologies can aid senior management to anticipate what could go wrong and the effects of potential events from both an internal and external perspective.

Leadership

The purpose of BCM leadership is to prepare the entire organization in advance of any major incident. It spearheads the implementation of the business continuity capability. Proactive leadership assures that organizational reputation and confidence are sustained following an incident. In addition, BCM leadership paves the way to a resilience culture across the organization, which could strengthen the position of BCM.

Governance

Corporate governance is a regulatory system that controls an organization and its activities. BCM forms an essential part of an organization's overall approach to governance. It establishes a programme of BCM activities in the organization and its supply network. It underpins the oversight capabilities that ensure controls are in place to protect key assets, earning capacity and the reputation of the organization.

Good business practice

BCM is good business management. It is about understanding the critical requirements of an organization. It identifies vulnerabilities in key processes and its supply chain, and develops BCM strategies to ensure that the organization is capable of meeting its business and statutory obligations.

Multidisciplinary function

BCM is a multidisciplinary function that encompasses the knowledge and skills of a diverse group of professionals to manage the corporate BCM programme. This multidisciplinary management process ensures that a broad range of threats is adequately identified and managed, thereby preserving the well-being of an organization and its stakeholders.

Communication

BCM communication determines the patterns of interaction between different groups of stakeholders, both from within and outside the organization. It establishes a communication framework that fosters information sharing between decision-makers and key stakeholders, thereby strengthening relationships. It facilitates the decision-making process in the command and control structure during an incident. In addition, a fit-for-purpose communication framework improves the flow of information to parties who require it for managing the recovery process.

Value preservation

Through BCM, the organization remains in a good position to effectively manage the undesired consequences of an incident. It minimizes the impact of losses and preserves the overall corporate value. In addition, it serves to safeguard shareholder confidence in order to secure future growth in the market.

Adaptation

BCM is constantly adapting within the organization. It is a management instrument that bolsters organizational activities. It is continually transforming its role to meet new challenges in business. At board level, BCM can be adopted as a corporate tool that helps to improve the quality of strategic planning. On the other hand, it can integrate with operational processes like business re-engineering to improve performance and efficiency.

Application of business continuity management in corporate setting

The dynamics of today's business environment coupled with the endemic of natural/human-caused disasters constantly pose new challenges to the way organizations manage the resilience of their corporate assets and activities. It is no surprise that the concepts of BCM are already intricately intertwined with core business activities. The key motivators for such adoption are far ranging, from statutory compliance to business process engineering.

In many public and private organizations, resilience professionals and general staff alike still hold the traditional view that BCM is about operational management with a particular focus on the resumption of critical processes, such as information technology disaster recovery (ITDR) and workplace recovery. This consensus view about its recovery function has established BCM as an integral element in the day-to-day business activities. On the other hand, there are corporate strategists with a visionary perception that BCM is an enabler that, if applied in the organization's long-range planning, could enhance business performance. Such a diverse view of BCM demonstrates its versatility at different levels of management activities.

Broadly, BCM can be adopted at the strategic level or integrated in operational activities, though the latter is more commonly practised. However, key drivers, such as competitiveness, compliance and customers are pushing the BCM initiative up the board level. The following are some key organizational activities that can benefit from BCM:

- Process evaluation
- New product/service assessment
- Resources allocation
- Long-range planning
- Workplace location
- Enterprise risk management

Process evaluation

BCM can provide an in-depth analysis into the delivery system of an organization's products and services. In particular, the business impact analysis (BIA) is beneficial at each stage of the process to evaluate the impact of non-delivery during a disruption. It should be carried out on an end-to-end basis by mapping out the entire system of activities.

The analytical process is complemented by a risk assessment (RA), which identifies the threats, vulnerabilities and single points of failure from the production to the final delivery of the product or service. Such holistic process evaluation enables the development of alternative ways to enhance the resilience of the delivery system.

New product/service assessment

Similar to the process evaluation, BCM is a useful tool during the planning and development of a new product/service. In the inception stage, it can assess threats and impacts in the production lifecycle and determine the strategies required to strengthen operational continuity before the actual product/service is rolled out. This also enables senior executives to make decisions on building resilience in the development programme.

Resources allocation

BCM can be adopted to analyse how an organization utilize its corporate resources. It conducts a thorough analysis into business processes in order to identify areas where resources can be assigned to more productive utilization. It ensures that there are sufficient backup resources available to implement BCM strategies following an incident. Furthermore, it identifies the key resources that support critical businesses and develops measures to safeguard their availability.

Long-range planning

BCM challenges corporate assumptions about threats and uncertainties by introducing 'what-ifs'. It uses probable scenarios in the strategic management process, with particular emphasis on corporate survival, which conventional management disciplines cannot offer. This encourages adopting a holistic view when making corporate decisions. The incorporation of the concept of 'continuity' helps to improve the quality of planning and ensures the devised strategies are not incapacitated by unforeseen circumstances.

Workplace location

BCM can be adopted to inform the corporate decision on the selection of office location. It assesses each location in terms of the site risk characteristics and their implications on the delivery of key products and services. In addition, it determines the distance for separation of critical operations and the relocation strategies if the primary site is affected by an incident.

Enterprise risk management

Enterprise risk management (ERM) manages the full spectrum of risks and their combined impact as an interrelated risk profile to the organization; incorporating BCM can underpin the risk management process. For instance, the activity of business impact analysis (BIA) offers the 'impact over time' dimension, which could uncover additional information on the characteristics of the identified risks and issues not previously considered.

Business continuity management lifecycle

BCM is a progressive and cyclical process. The framework described here draws on the key approaches generally adopted in the BCM industry. It is broadly divided into six interrelating components:

1 BCM programme management

2 Organizational and business analysis

3 Strategy selection and development

4 Incident management structure and plans development

5 Exercise, maintenance and review

6 Business continuity culture

Prior to the implementation of a BCM initiative, it is important to gain executive management agreement on the proposed BCM approach in the organization. This ensures that the initial project is adequately resourced and given the right emphasis that is accepted by all levels of the organization.

BCM programme management

BCM programme management establishes the organization's framework of developing and managing an adequate business continuity capability. This component provides the oversight of the entire BCM lifecycle. In broad terms, it consists of the following elements:

- BCM corporate alignment
- Programme scope
- Business continuity policy
- Roles, responsibilities and authorities
- Project management
- Programme management
- Documentation

BCM corporate alignment

Like other major management functions that support business performance, BCM provides the capability to effectively respond to incidents in order that the organization can fulfil its objectives and obligations. The BCM programme should align with the organization's business strategies and goals. This ensures that the programme is not a 'bolt-on' initiative but one that can effectively serve its intended purpose of expediting the recovery process whilst minimizing the impact of losses caused by a disruption. BCM should be viewed as a strategic initiative that contributes to the organization's long-term success. It should be recognized as a corporate planning tool for making strategic decisions.

Programme scope

The scope defines which areas of business in the organization are included in the BCM programme. The management decision is often based on the criticality of the products and services, such as those that account for a significant proportion of business revenue. It can also be based on the findings of the business impact analysis (BIA).

It is important to note that all outsourced activities that support the delivery of the in-scope products or services are to be included in the BCM programme since the overall responsibility of product and service delivery resides with the host organization. In most cases, the business areas that are excluded from the scope are managed by risk-mitigation measures.

From the management point of view, scoping is a tactical approach of ensuring a manageable BCM programme at the outset: a staged implementation of the BCM initiative. This approach allows the programme to be introduced in key areas of business, and it eventually expands across other parts of the organization. This is particularly useful for large organizations with diverse locations or those with limited resource capacity.

Business continuity policy

The business continuity policy is a high-level document that is owned by executive management. It is a formal statement that sets out the purpose of BCM in the organization. It reflects the business continuity objectives and is aligned with other key policies and strategies, notably, enterprise risk management. The document clearly defines the governance of the BCM programme, that is, the operating framework of establishing and managing the programme.

Roles, responsibilities and authorities

The BCM programme needs to be adequately resourced in order to remain responsive to business needs. Executive commitment assures the programme is sufficiently funded and secures a future for BCM. It is important to have the BCM initiative led by a senior figure who acts as the business continuity champion. This high-level role reinforces management support for BCM in the organization.

As an integral component of the BCM programme, the establishment of the organization's incident management structure requires various roles to be assigned to competent individuals based on knowledge, skills and experience. Depending on the size and complexity of an organization, the management structure could comprise specialized teams to manage the BCM programme.

In general, there are two phases in the BCM programme: programme management and incident management. The roles and responsibilities during the two phases vary significantly. In most cases, those who are responsible for managing the BCM programme will be called upon to assume duties during the incident phase since they have an intimate knowledge of the business continuity plans and procedures.

Project management

Ideally, the development of a BCM programme should follow a typical BCM lifecycle similar to the approach described in this book. However, the scope and extent of the BCM activities to be implemented is dependent upon the current state of BCM maturity in individual organizations.

In most cases, when the business continuity policy is approved, a series of activities in the form of projects are rolled out to establish the BCM programme. Each of these projects should be adequately scheduled and resourced. For instance, timescale, tasks, staff involved and deliverables need to be determined when undertaking a BIA project. Once the key components of BCM have been established, the project becomes programme; it is then managed on an ongoing basis.

Taking BCM programme development as a series of mini-projects is particularly useful when presenting progress updates to executive management. The regular supply of achievements in the form of deliverables at each stage of the project helps to secure management interest and support.

Programme management

The BCM programme is managed in accordance with the framework contained in the business continuity policy. It is a continuous and progressive cycle that requires managerial, operational, administrative and technical supports of the programme. Its long-term objective is to improve the business continuity capability of the organization. Two factors are crucial in the success of BCM programme management, namely, executive management support and staff support. The former is generally in the form of ongoing funding for the programme. In contrast, the latter refers to staff contribution through participation and training. Collectively, they reflect the organizational commitment to BCM.

It is important to note that the BCM programme does not remain stagnant. Corporate change drivers and dynamics of the wider environment require regular reviews of the BCM strategies and processes. It is the primary responsibility of the BCM team to ensure that different components of the programme remain adequate to meet corporate challenges.

Documentation

Due to the number of documents and records generated by the programme of BCM activities, the management of documents can be an overwhelming task. The purpose of establishing a documentation system is to demonstrate that the BCM programme is effectively managed. It should be designed and implemented in a consistent manner to support operational (incident response) and assessment (audit and review) requirements.

Documentation control helps to safeguard against unauthorized modification or loss of integrity of the documents. It ensures that authorized personnel have access to the most up-to-date plans during an incident. Another key motive is to provide the audit trail of the BCM processes; this is particularly important for organizations that are seeking certification to industry standards.

Organizational and business analysis

This component forms the basis of the entire BCM programme. It provides an in-depth review of the organization's structure and its processes. It identifies the threats within business, with particular focus on value-creating activities, and understands the impact of their non-availability over time on the organization. Organizational and business analysis consists of three complementary tools to determine the investment of the organization's BCM efforts:

- Business impact analysis
- Business continuity resource requirements analysis
- Risk assessment

Business impact analysis

The business impact analysis (BIA) is an objective approach that assesses the organizational activities whose failure would most immediately threaten product and service delivery and have significant impacts on the organization.

At the corporate level, the BIA can be used to determine the scope of the BCM programme, such as high-value products and services that could influence future growth. On the other hand, at the process level, the BIA assesses the undesired consequences of the failure of activities that can seriously jeopardize business performance over time. This is quantified in tangible and intangible terms, which include the loss of operating resources and time, financial losses, reputational damage and regulatory breaches.

In cases where the scope of the BCM programme has been determined, the BIA can be used to validate that all internal and external dependencies in relation to in-scope activities are included in the programme. The BIA should be carried out in an end-to-end business product and service context and not as independent lines of activities since the delivery process is intricately supported by a network of activities.

Business continuity resource requirements analysis

The business continuity resource requirements analysis (BCRRA) forms part of the BIA. Its purpose is to collect information on the minimum resources required to continue critical operations at an acceptable level. These include people, premises, information, technology and supplies that are crucial in fulfilling corporate objectives and obligations. The combined information of the BIA and the BCRRA is used as the basis for the formulation of BCM strategies.

Risk assessment

As an integrative part of organizational and business analysis, the risk assessment (RA) conducts an in-depth review to uncover vulnerability and exposure of the organizational activities to specific types of risk. Based on the RA, conceivable risks are prioritized in accordance to the corporate risk appetite and are used to inform the use of mitigation controls to manage their likelihood and impact.

There are many forms of risk management methodologies to support the BCM programme, some of which are developed for certain industries while others are adaptable to meet the general needs of business. In most cases, risk assessment methodologies encapsulate the basic principles of identification, evaluation, mitigation, and monitoring and review.

Strategy selection and development

Strategy selection and development entails the selection of an appropriate BCM strategy for each critical product and service, along with the development of process continuity solutions. Its purpose is to establish responses to maintain the continuity of critical operation at an acceptable level. In addition, the consolidation of recovery resources supports the formulation of continuity solutions. Strategy selection and development comprise three stages:

- Strategy options evaluation and selection
- Process continuity responses
- Consolidation of recovery resources

Strategy options evaluation and selection

The objective of evaluation and selection is to determine the BCM strategy that is able to support the recovery needs of each critical product and service. This is an in-depth evaluative process that is based on a number of factors, such as business requirements, costs of implementing the strategies compared to the speed of recovery, recovery phase (partial or full resumption) and consequences of inactions.

Process continuity responses

Continuity solutions are formulated according to the requirements of the chosen BCM strategy for each product and service. In most cases, continuity solutions are dictated by the availability of resources, namely, people, premises, technological infrastructures and critical supplies, which collectively form the key supports for an effective implementation.

Consolidation of recovery resources

The consolidation of recovery resources is an important aspect of the BCM programme. This activity re-evaluates all the resources needed to implement the organization's BCM strategies and continuity solutions. It ensures that the resources required to support the selected process continuity solutions are consistent and do not conflict with one another. It also enables purchasing leverage when acquiring resources and services from specialist suppliers.

Incident management structure and plans development

The development of an incident management structure (IMS) is to provide an organized framework with clear procedures for communication, command and control during an incident. Different levels of plans are formulated to support various teams in the incident management structure. Collectively, the structure and plans form the organizational response that enables business to continue at an acceptable level. This component is made up of two elements:

- Incident command and control structure
- Plans development

Incident command and control structure

An effective IMS should be simple and capable of the following:

- Confirming the nature and extent of the incident
- Taking control of the incident
- Containing the incident
- Communicating with stakeholders

Broadly, the IMS comprises three levels of management activities: strategic, tactical and operational. Each assumes different roles and responsibilities during an incident. Regardless of what operating structure an organization adopts, the fundamental principle is fit-for-purpose and provides clear procedures on the escalation and dissemination of information to various response teams and stakeholders.

Plan development

The objective of plan development is to formulate criteria and procedures to equip response teams with necessary guidance in managing an incident. Depending on the nature and complexity of an organization, there could be a diverse range of response plans with specific focus on different aspects of an incident. Similar to the IMS, these plans are broadly grouped into strategic, tactical and operational. Each plan contains pertinent information about the nature of the incident, the management process and a set of assumptions that together enable the teams to make prompt decisions.

In general, there are three levels of plans:

- Strategic level: crisis management plan
- Tactical level: business continuity plan
- Operational level: process recovery plan

Strategic level: crisis management plan The strategic plan, commonly called crisis management plan (CMP), is a high-level plan that contains the organization's overall business continuity strategy and a summary of all other plans. The CMP is used by executive management in addressing strategic issues of the incident. The threats covered by the CMP are not necessarily the conventional physical failure or damage of properties. In most cases, they are beyond the scope of the business continuity plan. The plan is usually invoked when impending crisis situations pose threats to the reputation or confidence of the organization, which could result in long-term damage to its business performance.

Tactical level: business continuity plan The business continuity plan (BCP) is an action-orientated document. It contains an integrated set of guidance that lays out the procedures of managing the continuity of operation. It enables the BCM team to assess the situation and galvanize the recovery resources in order to implement the appropriate strategies.

For small single-site organizations, the BCP can be a single document that contains simple procedures that address the recovery needs of critical processes; for multi-site organizations, the BCP could be a collection of plans. For the latter, the BCP facilitates and resolves any issues pertaining to the coordinated implementation of these plans.

Operational level: process recovery plan　Depending on the nature, scale and complexity of the organization and business processes, there could be a process recovery plan (PRP) that covers the individual product/service line of business, or a series of plans owned by business functions in which they are related. The PRP details actions and resources required to resume the critical process according to its target timescale and operational level.

Though plans contain solutions and procedures to achieve their recovery objectives, they are not intended to address every eventuality because the nature of individual incidents varies. The response teams need to adapt actions according to the circumstances.

Exercise, maintenance and review

The BCM programme is constantly subject to internal and external drivers of change. In many cases, change prompts reviews to verify that the BCM strategies are adequate to support corporate objectives and requirements. The central tenet of this component is to ensure that the BCM programme remains current, complete and fit-for-purpose. This requires an ongoing commitment from across the organization coupled with a maintenance regime of exercise and audit. This component is made up of three elements:

- Exercise
- Maintenance
- Audit and quality assurance

Exercise

Exercise emphasizes two key areas: staff and plans. Its purpose is to enhance staff skills and confidence, and to assess the quality of planning (plans and procedures). It provides a platform for management capability to interact with technical, logistical and administrative activities. It uncovers inherent shortcomings in the plan, such as false assumptions or unrealistic recovery timescales. This is an excellent opportunity to involve all critical suppliers in the process, which helps to establish resilience in the supply chain network by reviewing the overall business continuity preparedness. A post-exercise review in the form of a debrief session is usually carried out to identify lessons learned and opportunities for improvements in the BCM arrangements. There are many types of exercises, ranging from orientations to full-scale exercises.

Maintenance

The dynamics of the organization and its wider environment can render the BCM programme obsolete. Maintenance ensures that the programme and its components remain in line with the organization's overall strategy. In most cases, maintenance is triggered by the results of exercises and audits. However, a review of the BCM programme is necessary when there are significant changes in corporate strategies or business processes.

Audit and quality assurance

Audit verifies that the BCM programme activities are adequately managed through conformance with the requirements set out in the business continuity policy or other relevant standards. Such conformance, if followed appropriately, could develop an effective business continuity capability. In contrast, quality assurance focuses on the BCM function within the organization. It establishes a series of key performance indicators (KPIs) to monitor and evaluate the efficiency of BCM in the organization. It uses the KPIs to appraise staff and key activities in the BCM programme. Examples of KPIs include the number of training courses attended by each member of the BCM team and the number of exercises carried out in the past 12 months.

Business continuity culture

Creating a business continuity culture within the organization should be an essential part of the BCM programme. It involves the integration of BCM principles across all levels of management activities. Staff should understand its importance in safeguarding the organization's critical businesses and their contribution to the achievement of its intended outcomes. In turn, this leads to the growth of the BCM maturity. This component comprises two aspects:

- Developing business continuity awareness
- Maintaining business continuity culture

Developing business continuity awareness

Raising awareness is the first step in the development of a corporate resilience culture. This entails the communication of the need for BCM and actively promoting its benefits across the organization. A series of awareness campaigns for specific audiences is an effective approach to drive the BCM initiative. It is important to note that promoting the business continuity cultural awareness also extends to critical suppliers and other external stakeholders that are an integral part of the organization's delivery network.

Maintaining business continuity culture

Maintaining the business continuity culture is an ongoing commitment. This should be supported by awareness and training programmes. Awareness programmes are designed for staff who do not have specific duties in the BCM programme. The purpose is to raise their understanding about BCM and how it relates to their job responsibilities. In contrast, training programmes aim to upgrade the knowledge and skills of those tasked with managing the BCM programme. This entails the improvement of their management capability in different phases of BCM, that is, programme management and incident response. Collectively, these programmes help to create a positive cultural shift for BCM and entrench the subject in corporate culture.

Figure 1.1 outlines the business continuity management lifecycle.

FIGURE 1.1 Business continuity management lifecycle

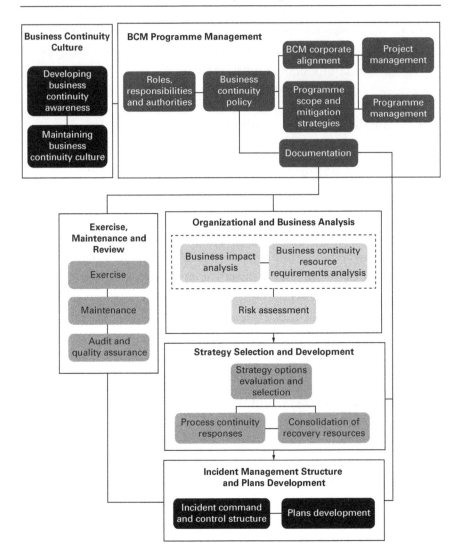

Summary

The conventional view has seen BCM as an operational discipline for protecting the organization's critical processes. However, the versatility of the subject coupled with the benefits it brings to board-level planning has enhanced its role as a strategic instrument. It is well-known that for any initiative to achieve a lasting effect in the organization, executive management support is paramount. Experiences so far have shown that corporate leadership plays a significant role in embedding business continuity culture across the organization. Although having full organizational support and an established business continuity culture are considered a big leap for BCM, the ultimate success of the BCM programme is dependent on those who manage the activities. As such, due emphasis should be given to develop the skills of staff with specific BCM responsibilities.

CHECKLIST

This checklist is intended to support the business continuity management system (BCMS) development process	Yes	No	Action required
Has the senior leadership team articulated a workable definition of BCM?	☐	☐	☐
Does the organization accept the importance of a BCM programme within the corporate governance structure?	☐	☐	☐
Is BCM connected to the corporate objectives of the organization?	☐	☐	☐
Are the principles of BCM incorporated in the organizational activities?	☐	☐	☐
Is the organization able to establish a BCM programme and its processes to safeguard the critical activities?	☐	☐	☐

References

ISO 22301:2012 – Societal security – Business continuity management systems – Requirements

Further reading

Bird, L (2011) *Dictionary of Business Continuity Management Terms*, Business Continuity Institute, Caversham

Business Continuity Institute (2013) *Good Practice Guidelines: A guide to global good practice in business continuity*, Business Continuity Institute, Caversham

Disaster Recovery Institute International (DRII) (2012) *Professional Practices for Business Continuity Practitioners*, DRII, New York

Disaster Recovery Institute International (2013) *International Glossary for Resiliency*, DRII, New York

Business continuity management system

02

OVERVIEW

- This chapter explains what a management system is and highlights the different levels of application.
- It goes on to introduce ISO 22301 – Business Continuity Management System (BCMS) and its fundamental roles.
- It describes the key components that make up the BCMS and explains their individual features.
- It discusses the concepts of the Plan-Do-Check-Act (PDCA) paradigm and how the four phases operate in the BCMS.
- Finally, the chapter provides an overview of the BCMS lifecycle and outlines the main elements that establish the business continuity capability.

Background

Management systems in the areas of quality, security, risk and environmental management have significantly shaped the way organizations meet their management challenges and attend to stakeholder requirements. The purpose of any ISO management system is to enable organizations to improve the effectiveness of existing processes. This is bolstered by an iterative and flexible systems paradigm: Plan-Do-Check-Act (PDCA) cycle. The PDCA paradigm offers a structured approach to address the organization's needs. It identifies corporate deficiencies and develops actions to improve the effectiveness of management capability.

Such management effectiveness should be driven by the senior leadership team. A management system is an effective way to gain executive commitment. In particular, most international standards recommend senior leadership participation. Equally important is the support from the organization's functions and critical suppliers to ensure that processes of the management system are implemented consistently.

The launch of ISO 22301, Societal Security – Business Continuity Management Systems – Requirements, reflects the importance of business continuity management (BCM) in safeguarding productive capability and stakeholder interests. Like other management systems, the business continuity management system (BCMS) is about developing, implementing and managing a series of fit-for-purpose processes to achieve the requirements stipulated in the business continuity policy.

ISO 22301 is a universal approach to establishing an organization's BCMS. It guides organizations in the development of a holistic programme based on structured integration of best practice into their BCM activities. However, the key to implementing a BCMS effectively is often one that is aligned to the organization's corporate governance.

What is a management system?

In the broadest sense, a management system is an integrated set of processes and tools that an organization uses to develop its strategy, transform it into actions, and monitor and improve the effectiveness of management capability. This is a cyclical approach that streamlines an organization's activities, that is, systemizing its overall structure, planning processes, responsibilities and resources for developing, implementing and reviewing the objectives and policies.

From the management point of view, the corporate motivation for adopting a management system is diverse, from cost and time reduction to improvement of internal processes. Having a BCMS also demonstrates to key stakeholders that the organization is constantly seeking process optimization, effective risk management and innovation, which, as a whole, underpins corporate confidence.

In the longer term, its benefits to organizations include better resource allocation, improved risk management and increased customer satisfaction. Management systems are firmly grounded on the notion of disciplined management thinking and progressive improvement that drive organizational performance.

All international standards are based on the principle of continual improvement, an ongoing process that maintains the effectiveness and efficiency of the management system through regular reviews and improvements. This is bolstered by audits that assess the adequacy of key management activities.

Essentially, management systems need to be driven from board level. This ensures that they are given the correct level of emphasis and secure a better chance of successful implementation. A top-driven approach also helps to raise the corporate understanding of the management system and how its components apply in organizational activities. Over time, this could lead to it becoming part of the organization's mainstream management practice.

Many management systems are in the form of national and international standards, which are developed by leading practitioners in the field. The publication of such standards requires the majority approval of its members (for national standards) and member bodies (international standards). Likewise, this international standard for business continuity management systems is developed in such manner. Greater detail about the development process of management system standards are beyond the scope of this book.

Levels of application

Due to their generic features, most management systems can readily be incorporated into an organization's existing activities. At the outset of its implementation, it is important for executive management to define what the objectives and activities are, and tailor them to corporate requirements.

In the broadest sense, management systems can be progressively applied in three levels – from basic introduction of the BCMS concepts leading to the certification of the BCMS (see Table 2.1).

TABLE 2.1 Three levels of management system application

Level	Objective	Activity/Assessment
1	Develop an **awareness** of the subject	• Introduce the concepts of the standard in the management processes. • The assessment is in the form of internal audits (also known as first-party audits) that are conducted by the organization for management review and other internal purposes.
2	Establish a **compliance culture** of the standard	• Develop and incorporate an ongoing management framework (based on the specified principles of the standard) in the management processes. • The assessment is conducted by parties having an interest in the organization, such as clients, or by agents engaged on their behalf. This is called supplier audit, also known as second-party audit.
3	Achieve a **certification** of the management system	• Establish a policy, objectives and a series of activities (in accordance to the requirements of the standard) in the management processes. • The assessment is conducted by independent auditing organizations or those providing certification. This is also called the third-party audit.

ISO 22301 – business continuity management system

ISO 22301, the world's first international standard for BCM, has been developed to help organizations minimize the risk of disruptions. The publication of this standard reflects the growing consensus of the value that BCM contributes to organizational performance.

ISO 22301 brings together all existing standards and a collection of good practices to develop a universal approach to BCM. It emphasizes establishing a fit-for-purpose BCMS that is able to provide an effective response to disruptions and minimizes undesired impacts on the organization. This, however, requires management leadership and adequate resource support to manage the BCMS.

The BCMS specifies the requirements for setting up and managing an effective corporate business continuity capability. It provides guidance to enable an organization to optimize service availability in order to fulfil its objectives and obligations.

Broadly, the BCMS focuses on the following:

- Understanding the corporate requirements and incorporating these into the business continuity policy and objectives

- Implementing and operating actions for managing the corporate business continuity capability before and during disruptions

- Monitoring and reviewing the effectiveness of the BCMS

- Continual improvement of the BCMS

In an effort to align the BCMS to existing management processes, it is useful to integrate the principles of business continuity within the context of corporate governance. It can act as an internal control to manage risks in relation to both the decision-making process and day-to-day running of the organization.

ISO 22301 comprises 13 sections with two supporting sections: Foreword and Bibliography. The first four sections: Introduction, Scope, Normative References and Terms and Definitions, are considered informative. The proceeding seven sections – namely, Context of the Organization, Leadership, Planning, Support, Operation, Performance Evaluation and Improvement – form the essence of the BCMS lifecycle. This international standard is one of the first to adopt this new format, which subsequent management system standards will follow. This maintains consistency amongst management system standards as well as integrating with standards already in the organization.

Following the publication of the BCMS requirements (ISO 22301), its counterpart, ISO 22313, was launched. The purpose of ISO 22313 is to provide further explanation on the ISO 22301 clauses and their intents. Furthermore, the guidance reflects the global management experience and good practice of BCM. In addition to the knowledge and experience of the authors, this book also encapsulates principles contained in ISO 22313 and other good BCM practice concepts available elsewhere.

Though the adoption of ISO 22301 is optional, incorporating its concepts can be beneficial to those organizations with the following motivations:

- Develop and establish the BCMS with a constant driver of improvement
- Conform with the organizational business continuity policy and objectives
- Demonstrate to key stakeholders the adoption and compliance to ISO 22301
- Third-party certification of the organizational BCMS to ISO 22301

It is worth noting that the requirements specified in ISO 22301 are generic and can be applied to public and private organizations, regardless of type, size and nature. The extent of application is also dependent on the organization's operating environment and complexity.

Key components of business continuity management system

In broad terms, the BCMS comprises a number of key components:

- Business continuity policy
- Defined roles and responsibilities
- BCMS management processes
- Documentation
- Other relevant BCM processes

Business continuity policy

In most cases, BCM documentation has some form of hierarchy. At the top of this documentary structure sits the business continuity policy. This high-level document establishes the purpose of BCMS, that is, the objectives, principles and requirements of the BCMS. It provides an overview of how the BCMS operates in the organization. It defines the scope of the management system and ensures that BCM activities are aligned with corporate requirements and regulations. The policy also reflects management commitment to the BCMS.

Defined roles and responsibilities

Like any management programme, there should be staff with dedicated roles and responsibilities to implement and manage the BCMS. In most cases, the size of the management team is dependent upon the nature of the organization, which may be managed using a virtual management structure or reporting lines. It is important that participation is adequately represented to reflect the organization's main functions and corporate interests.

BCMS management processes

The BCMS comprises a series of interrelating management processes established to achieve the business continuity objectives. Though the management processes can be carried out independently, they should be viewed as a joined-up system. This encourages the organization to adopt a holistic approach to managing the BCMS. In essence, the main processes of the BCMS include the following:

- **Policy formulation** – The purpose is to develop a business continuity policy that sets out an operating framework for BCMS. The policy includes the objectives, processes and guiding principles that are aligned to organizational requirements.
- **Development and management** – At the development stage of the BCMS, a series of progressive activities are planned and implemented to achieve the project outcomes. It is then

transformed into a management programme that requires ongoing maintenance and improvement.

- **Performance evaluation** – This process is about analyzing the adequacy of the business continuity capability using defined targets and performance indicators. It also helps to determine appropriate actions to rectify deficiencies in the BCMS.

- **Management review** – This is a high-level appraisal of the BCMS performance based upon the results of the performance evaluation. The objective is to involve executive management in the BCMS, whilst ensuring that business continuity remains a board-level issue. Activities of the management review include authorizing actions and resources to improve the effectiveness of the BCMS performance.

- **Continual improvement** – The purpose of this process is to ensure that the BCMS operates effectively and remains relevant in its current context. In essence, the findings of the performance evaluation, together with actions of the management review, form the basis for continual improvement.

Documentation

Processes and procedures of the BCMS are documented in accordance to the organization's information guidelines or in compliance with the requirements of ISO 22301. Broadly, documentary materials include the business continuity policy, plans, reports and any others that pertain to addressing the requirements of the BCMS.

Other relevant BCM processes

Apart from the key processes mentioned earlier, a range of functions could be involved in the development of plans and processes to support the BCMS, which form an integral part of the overall business continuity capability. The following are some typical planning processes related to BCM:

- **Pandemic preparedness** – This is part of the health and safety consideration that addresses the welfare of staff and is usually carried out by respective departments working in conjunction with BCM and human resources functions to prevent widespread illnesses and impacts within the organization. Pandemic preparedness ensures that key staff are available to deliver the critical activities.

- **Succession planning** – The purpose of succession planning is to minimize impacts due to the unavailability of key staff. It can be broadly defined as the process of identifying the knowledge and skills that are required to perform critical activities. This safeguards the management capability of individuals who make key decisions and those responsible for undertaking highly customized activities. Some common approaches of succession planning include multiskill training programmes and the documentation of key skills and ways in which critical activities are performed.

- **Information technology disaster recovery (ITDR)/information security (IS)** – In broad terms, ITDR and IS cover a spectrum of activities, ranging from the planning for recovery of simple data-processing capability to preservation of information security. Given the advancement of new technologies, as well as emergence of new security threats, the planning process can be far-ranging, depending on the organizational requirements.

- **Crisis communication** – This process preserves the organization's shareholder value and long-term reputation following a crisis situation. It entails the development of communication strategies for different stakeholder groups to maintain confidence and demonstrate the organization's business continuity capability.

- **Workplace recovery** – Workplace recovery addresses the organization's premises and facilities management issues. It determines strategies to safeguard the primary workplace against probable threats as well as arrangements to relocate critical activities to an alternate site.

- **Logistics and supply chain management** – The maintenance of an inventory of critical supplies is an essential part of BCM. The process develops backup strategies for key suppliers and stocks to underpin resilience in the supply chain.

The Plan-Do-Check-Act (PDCA) paradigm

At the heart of ISO 22301 is a driver that optimizes the processes in the BCMS. This driver, also known as the Plan-Do-Check-Act (PDCA) paradigm, is fundamental to any management system. The paradigm ensures that organizations can effectively complete the full cycle of the management system, thereby achieving its intended outcomes.

In essence, the PDCA paradigm consists of four generic phases in a management system:

- Plan
  - Identify and assess issues in management processes
  - Define the scope of the organization's management system: policies, objectives, processes and procedures
  - Select control objectives and controls that will address these issues
  - Prepare the Statement of Applicability (SoA) documenting the controls selected and justifying any decisions not to implement or only to partially implement certain controls
- Do
  - Formulate and implement a management plan with actions
  - Implement the previously selected controls to meet the control objectives
- Check
  - Conduct periodic reviews to validate the effectiveness of the management system
  - Appraise the processes against defined requirements and objectives of the policy
  - Periodically conduct internal management system audits

- Act

  - Implement devised management system improvements
  - Take appropriate corrective and preventive actions
  - Maintain communication with key stakeholders
  - Validate improvements

The PDCA paradigm cycle is widely recognized as a process-centric approach. It uses activities such as feedback loops and controls to establish methods of improvement or devise appropriate management processes for the organization. It is also effective as a process-optimization tool that offers the following advantages:

- It can easily be integrated in existing management activities and fosters continuous improvement to processes and procedures.

- It helps to identify a range of new solutions to resolve existing problems by trial testing in a controlled manner and selecting the most appropriate solutions prior to full implementation.

- It supports better utilization of organizational resources in the processes, thereby minimizing wastages and improving the efficiency of the entire system.

- It encourages an approach for systems thinking. This simple cycle adopts a holistic view in the development of appropriate solutions to enhance process efficiency of the management system.

In this context, the four phases of the paradigm can be incorporated into the key processes of the BCMS.

Plan – Establish the BCMS

The rationale of the Plan phase is to align the BCMS to support the organization's goals and strategies. This phase establishes the operating framework for the BCMS. It identifies the key management issues that define the focus, that is, the scope of the BCMS. A critical component of this phase is to gain executive support to implement the BCMS within the organization. The Plan phase comprises four components: Context of the Organization, Leadership, Planning and Support.

Do – Implement and Operate the BCMS

This phase implements the BCMS in accordance to the requirements of the business continuity policy. The Do phase consists of Operation.

Check – Monitor and Review the BCMS

The Check phase assesses the effectiveness of the BCMS against requirements of the business continuity policy. Appropriate tools and methods are adopted to evaluate the adequacy of BCM activities. The results are reviewed by executive management, which then devise authorized actions to improve the BCMS performance. The Check phase consists of Performance Evaluation.

Act – Maintain and Improve the BCMS

The Act phase determines potential issues pertaining to the management of the BCMS, which are then incorporated into the Plan phase. This entails the review of the business continuity policy, objectives and requirements. The Act phase consists of Improvement.

Details of individual components in each phase are further explained in the respective chapters of this book. Table 2.2 provides an overview of the PDCA phases as they relate to the components of the BCMS.

Business continuity management system lifecycle

In essence, the BCMS lifecycle is made up of the following components:

- Context of the organization
- Leadership

TABLE 2.2 PDCA phases and BCMS components

PDCA Phases	Components
Plan (Establish the BCMS)	• Context of the organization (Chapter 3) • Leadership (Chapter 4) • Planning (Chapter 5) • Support (Chapter 6)
Do (Implement and operate the BCMS)	• Operation (Chapter 7)
Check (Monitor and review the BCMS)	• Performance evaluation (Chapter 8)
Act (Maintain and improve the BCMS)	• Improvement (Chapter 9)

- Planning
- Support
- Operation
- Performance evaluation
- Improvement

Context of the organization

Context of the organization sets the scene for the development of the BCMS. The process identifies the internal and external drivers that are relevant to the organization. These drivers are then used as requirements to outline the BCMS context. This component also highlights the importance of undertaking an in-depth stakeholder and regulatory analysis. It helps to understand the implications that could impact the organization's BCMS. In most cases, this takes the form of risks and opportunities. Depending on the nature of the organization and the environment in which it operates, other relevant factors that could affect the scoping (context) of the BCMS should also be incorporated in the process. Context of the organization can be broken into four elements:

- Understanding of the organization and its context
- Understanding the needs and expectations of interested parties
- Determining the scope of the management system
- Business continuity management system

Leadership

Leadership stresses the importance of executive support for the BCMS. It stipulates management commitment towards the BCMS and how executive management articulate their expectations via the policy statement. Central to this component is the development of the business continuity policy and the role of the senior leadership team in establishing various aspects of the BCM structure, namely, roles, responsibilities and authorities; working groups; and modes of communication. Leadership consists of the following elements:

- Leadership and commitment
- Management commitment
- Policy
- Organizational roles, responsibilities and authorities

Planning

This component establishes the actions that are required to address key management issues, namely, risks and opportunities, which could affect the organization's business continuity capability. These actions are developed into business continuity objectives and aligned to corporate goals and strategies. In addition, planning sets out the blueprint for implementing the BCMS project. This component is made up of two elements:

- Actions to address risks and opportunities
- Business continuity objectives and plans to achieve them

Support

Support lays out the foundation of planning and managing the BCMS. It highlights the importance of organizational resources and staff competence for establishing an effective BCMS. This is coupled by an established awareness and training programme that helps to integrate BCM in the organization's activities. It is important that the entire BCMS is underpinned by an appropriate incident communication structure that sets out the process of disseminating information to internal and external stakeholders before, during and after an incident. In addition, the BCM team need to ensure that there is a documentation management system to regulate control and management of business continuity materials. Support consists of five elements:

- Resources
- Competence
- Awareness
- Communication
- Documented information

Operation

This component consists of a range of activities that establish the BCMS. It places emphasis on advance planning and preparation that are necessary to ensure the continuity of critical operations in the event of an incident. It identifies impacts and threats to organizational functions and formulates BCM strategies. It also states the importance of establishing a fit-for-purpose incident management structure, supported by appropriate plans and procedures. This is reinforced by exercises and testing that validates plans and procedures as well as the individual/collective capability. This component comprises five elements:

- Operational planning and control
- Business impact analysis and risk assessment
- Business continuity strategy

- Establishment and implementation of business continuity procedures
- Exercising and testing

Performance evaluation

Performance evaluation appraises the BCMS performance. As an integral part of the BCMS, this component establishes a monitoring and management programme to ensure the BCMS remains effective. This is followed by management review that assesses opportunities for improvement and the requirements for changes to the BCMS. This process entails the authorization of actions related to improving the effectiveness of the BCMS. Performance evaluation comprises three elements:

- Monitoring, measurement, analysis and evaluation
- Internal audit
- Management review

Improvement

Improvement focuses on the ongoing enhancement of the BCMS. Predominantly, it identifies nonconformities in the BCMS and formulates actions to adjust existing processes that are not functioning to specified requirements. Though the purpose of continual improvement is to eliminate causes of deviations and ensure compliance with the necessary guidelines, it also provides opportunities to optimize the BCMS. Improvement consists of two elements:

- Nonconformity and corrective action
- Continual improvement

Figure 2.1 depicts the relationship between the BCMS (with the PDCA paradigm) and the BCM lifecycle.

FIGURE 2.1 BCMS (with the PDCA paradigm) and BCM lifecycle

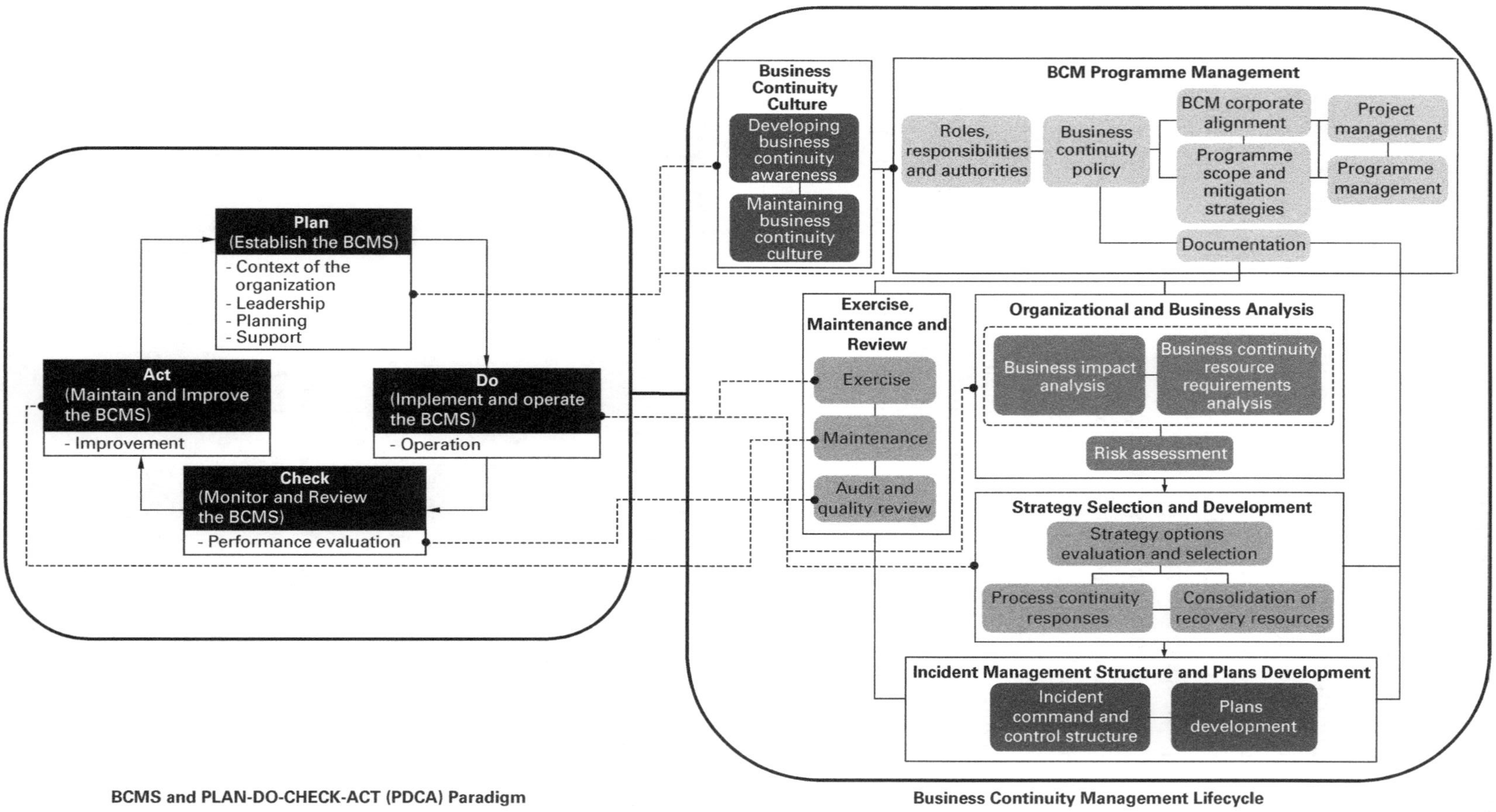

BCMS and PLAN-DO-CHECK-ACT (PDCA) Paradigm

Business Continuity Management Lifecycle

Summary

Formal management systems provide the means for organizations to improve internal controls and management competence. Their processes and procedures help to maintain organizational status quo and minimize downside risks. ISO 22301 is a flexible approach that provides organizations with the freedom to adopt the essential components that are most appropriate to their operating context. The distinctive characteristic of ISO 22301 is the incorporation of the PDCA phases in the BCMS lifecycle.

Adopting the BCMS optimizes the organization's business continuity capability. It provides organizations with an understanding of the management requirements and resource commitment necessary to achieve the business continuity objectives. More important, it emphasizes the involvement of executive management in the ongoing enhancement of the BCMS.

CHECKLIST

This checklist is intended to support the business continuity management system (BCMS) development process	Yes	No	Action required
Does the senior leadership team understand what a management system is and its benefits in enhancing management effectiveness?	☐	☐	☐
Has the senior leadership team determined the appropriate level of BCMS implementation within the organization?	☐	☐	☐
Does the organization's BCM programme incorporate the key components of the BCMS?	☐	☐	☐
Does the organization use the Plan-Do-Check-Act (PDCA) paradigm as an integral part of its BCM programme to optimize management processes and business continuity capability?	☐	☐	☐

Further reading

Business Continuity Institute (2013) *Good Practice Guidelines: A guide to global good practice in business continuity*, Business Continuity Institute, Caversham

Disaster Recovery Institute International (DRII) (2012) *Professional Practices for Business Continuity Practitioners*, DRII, New York

ISO 22300 (2012) – Societal security – Terminology

ISO 22301 (2012) – Societal security – Business continuity management systems – Requirements

ISO 22313 (2012) – Societal security – Business continuity management systems – Guidance

Further reading

Context of the organization

03

OVERVIEW

- This chapter first outlines the basic concepts of the organization and its wider environment.
- It then discusses the three components of organizational context analysis and describes their key activities.
- The chapter goes on to explain what an organizational BCMS scoping is and how to undertake a scoping activity.
- Finally, it highlights the implications when outsourcing the organization's functions and services.

Background

The organization is a complex system of activities made up of many interrelated functions. Its operation is constantly shaped by a range of internal and external drivers. As such, it is important to define and understand the key issues that can influence an organization's ability to achieve its objectives and obligations. Naturally, the process of understanding the organizational context is an integral part of the strategic planning process. In order to maintain growth and competitiveness, corporate leaders should be ready to take maximum advantage of the challenges presented whilst minimizing the uncertainties to the organization.

The incorporation of the BCMS in critical activities can help to protect business from potentially harmful events. Understanding the organizational context is a fundamental process of establishing the BCMS in the organization. The outputs from this process define the scope for the BCMS and form the basis of implementing the business continuity capability. This management system approach ensures that only organizational activities that contribute to the achievement of corporate goals are covered in the BCMS. It also reflects the participation of executive management in ensuring that the BCMS is aligned with the strategic requirements of the organization.

Understanding the organizational context

The development of the organization's BCMS is a project in its own right and must be undertaken rigorously. The first stage comprises the identification of internal and external drivers that could affect business performance. These drivers are assessed and taken into account when designing the BCMS. Identifying the key drivers forms the first component of the Plan phase of the PDCA paradigm, which consists of organizational context analysis and organizational BCMS scoping.

Basic concepts: The organization and its environment

The environment in which the organization operates is a dynamic system that is fused with uncertainty and volatility. It is essential for the organization to undertake a holistic review of the wider environment in order to develop an understanding of its relationship with various environmental drivers and how their effects impact the objectives, strategies and operating activities. Equally important, an internal review of the organizational system provides an in-depth understanding of the relationship between various corporate components and how they contribute to the achievement of corporate goals. From the business continuity perspective, these reviews piece together a big picture of the challenges to the organizational activities that support the delivery of critical products and services. They collectively form the basis of developing the BCMS.

Figure 3.1 depicts the relationship between the environmental and organizational systems. This is a simplistic illustration to help readers understand the basic concepts of the organization's interaction with its environment. In reality, the interaction is more intricate.

FIGURE 3.1 Interaction between internal and external systems

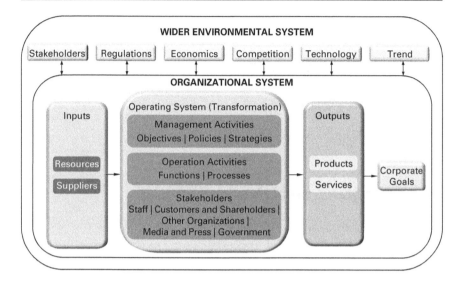

Organizational context analysis

The purpose of analysing the organizational context is to identify and evaluate the key drivers that impact the organization's value-creating activities. Their implications are useful in defining the scoping requirements for the BCMS. Organizational context analysis is broadly divided into three areas, namely, corporate analysis, threat and resilience assessment, and stakeholder and regulatory analysis. Table 3.1 summarizes the three components of the organizational context analysis.

TABLE 3.1 Components of organizational context analysis

Components	Activities
Corporate Analysis	• Corporate goals, objectives and policies • Processes and resources
Threat and Resilience Assessment	• Identify threats and impacts • Assess corporate preparedness
Stakeholder and Regulatory Analysis	• Stakeholders • Regulatory compliance

Corporate analysis

Corporate analysis focuses on the management approach that enables the organization to achieve its business aspirations. This includes assembling all relevant facts about the following:

- Corporate goals, objectives and policies
- Processes and resources

Corporate goals, objectives and policies

Organizations exist with a purpose to perform certain activities. The overall purpose is translated into goals that are the driving force for their existence. These goals are developed into corporate objectives and are documented in organizational policies. An understanding of the following elements ensures that the BCMS appropriately supports the business requirements.

- Goals – Most organizations should have some form of goals about the expected outcomes of the business. These goals can be embodied in a formal statement such as the organization's overall mission statement. They determine the type of business, namely, inputs (resources), outputs (products and services) and key processes.

- Objectives – Objectives set out what needs to be performed in order to achieve the expected outcomes. These objectives are generally related to the goals that are defined in the organization's strategic plan.

- Policies – Policy documents are developed in accordance to the framework of objectives. They generally include organizational guidelines, performance standards, enterprise risk management and statutory requirements. They provide the basis for the development of strategies to achieve the objectives.

Processes and resources

The delivery of the organization's products and services is undertaken by various subsystems, also known as functions. The functions perform their unique transformation process that converts 'in' resources into the next level of output, which can take place within the organization or its delivery system.

The management team needs to identify the key functions in order to understand how their activities are managed as a whole towards achieving corporate goals. In the broadest sense, organizational functions are made up of processes and resources that comprise the following elements:

1 Processes and procedures – Organizational processes are documented as work procedures that inform how specific tasks are carried out with regards to the delivery of the products and services. They are commonly in the forms of operations manuals and guidelines that specify service levels, quality and technical requirements.

2 Assets and resources – Business performance is dependent on the effective utilization of assets and resources. They are crucial in supporting the organization's management and operational activities. Broadly, they are classified into six areas:

   – People – Determined roles and responsibilities based on knowledge and skills profiles.

   – Premises – This refers to buildings in the forms of offices or workplaces that support a range of organizational activities.

   – Infrastructures and systems – This refers to the equipment and technologies that support organizational activities to operate in a more efficient manner. In essence, they contribute to the transformation process in the organization's subsystems.

   – Suppliers – Specialist services offered by third parties can support the delivery of critical products and services or serve as support functions that enable the organization to focus on its primary activities.

- Supplies – These are the primary resources and stocks that provide 'input' to the transformation process.
- Reputation – This refers to the corporate image, brand and confidence that sustain the organization's business performance in the marketplace.

Threat and resilience assessment

The purpose of identifying and analyzing threats in respect of the organization's critical operations is to develop a profile of threats that can impede business performance. It should be undertaken as part of executive management's corporate planning activity. In addition, the introduction of gap analysis can determine the current level of corporate preparedness and define what actions are necessary to safeguard key businesses.

Identify threats and impacts

Organizational activities are exposed to innumerable threats that have the potential to compromise the achievement of corporate goals. From the business continuity perspective, this process provides three functions. First, it identifies and evaluates the inherent threats to critical processes. Second, the findings inform the development of an action plan, in this instance, a case for business continuity. Third, it helps to establish the scope for the BCMS.

As a starting point, a reference to the organization's risk register (if one is available) could provide an overall picture of the organization's risk landscape. Alternatively, conducting a high-level risk workshop with managers of major functions helps to uncover the key threats faced by the organization. This activity identifies the exposure of critical processes to specific types of threats and evaluates their impacts on business. It can also develop an understanding of the interdependencies amongst different functions in order to determine single points of failure or areas with high concentration of risk.

Assess corporate preparedness

The purpose of this activity is to determine the state of the organization's preparedness in its present context. This can be in the form of gap analysis, which identifies performance deficiencies in the corporate resilience capability and develops appropriate actions to address those issues that could impact the continuity of critical operations.

An initial review of policies and plans in the areas of business continuity, emergency and security, coupled with an in-depth discussion with the risk management function, can produce an overall impression of the organization's risk appetite and its outlook towards resilience planning.

Stakeholder and regulatory analysis

Prior to undertaking the BCMS scoping analysis, the organization should identify its key stakeholders and regulatory requirements that bear on its BCMS.

Stakeholders

Stakeholders are individuals or groups that have an interest in the organization's performance. They can be affected by its activities or its members' behaviours, or conversely, have the capacity to influence how the organization plans and manages its activities. Stakeholders are crucial to the development of a fit-for-purpose BCMS. Those affected or having the capacity to influence the outcome of the management system must be identified since the implementation and eventual management of the BCMS could trigger a wide range of reactions. As such, it is important for the BCM team to understand the requirements and impacts of all relevant stakeholders when establishing the BCMS. The following proposes a list of generic stakeholders who would or could be affected by the organization's BCMS:

- Staff
- Customers and shareholders

- Other organizations
- Media and press
- Government

Staff

At the outset, it is imperative to garner the board-level support for the BCMS, particularly the decision-makers who have the authority to approve budgets for corporate projects. However, it is equally important to gather feedback from those who potentially would be affected by or could affect the implementation of the BCMS. This includes general staff who work in key areas of business and those who have specific roles and responsibilities in managing incidents. Their collective participation has a significant impact on the organization's business continuity capability. It is also important to determine how the BCMS can influence the organization-wide staff in terms of their work activities.

Customers and shareholders

Customers and shareholders includes parties who consume the organization's products and services or those who have vested interest in its corporate performance; more essentially, their confidence can influence an organization's long-term success. It is important that the organization defines its responsibilities and obligations to this group of stakeholders.

Other organizations

In the broadest sense, this comprises competitors, suppliers and client organizations that the organization is bound to by contractual relationships.

- Competitors – Though competitors are generally rival organizations operating in the same market, the organization needs to take into account the implications of a systemic failure that could affect the industry and how organizations as a whole respond to a sector-wide incident.

- Suppliers – Engaging third-party suppliers can reduce costs and provide a business benefit. However, from the business continuity perspective, third-party arrangements pose risks if key suppliers fail to fulfil their obligations due to unforeseen circumstances. It is important that the host organization identifies such risks in its delivery system and ensures that necessary resilience arrangements are built into the supply chain.

- Client organizations – This refers to client organizations to which the organization is bound by contractual terms to supply particular products or services. The intricate interdependencies of these organizations often mean that a sudden disruption in the supply chain could cause a series of triggering effects. In most cases, the impacts of failure are compounded, and organizations along the network are affected to varying degrees dependent on their level of business continuity preparedness. Most of these organizations are operating in energy, utilities, communications, food, health care and financial services industries. Though there could be imposed financial penalties in contractual terms, certain costs incurred are beyond financial quantifications, such as confidence and reputation.

Media and press

The actions of the media and press have a profound impact on the long-term performance, or in some cases, the viability of an organization. In crisis situations, news about an organization and its management behaviour will inevitably come to the spotlight, which can shape the perceptions of the audience, chiefly, customers and shareholders. As such, it is useful to seek media advice on the development of crisis communication strategies to address the information requirements of key stakeholders.

Government

Most government policies have direct influences on how organizations shape their business strategies and plans. Organizations are obliged to adhere to the regulations imposed by the national regulators in their specific industries. Non-compliance can often lead to undesirable outcomes, not to mention the public attention fuelled by the indiscriminate reporting of the media and press.

In order to assess the level of stakeholder influence, a simple matrix table can be constructed to establish individual stakeholder characteristics based on interest, control, position and impact around the organization's BCMS (Table 3.2).

Regulatory compliance

Regulatory compliance has always been a challenge to organizations since it has a significant influence on corporate planning. In recent years, we have witnessed new national legislations around the world that impose business continuity requirements, whether mandatory or optional, on public and private organizations. As the benefits of business continuity are becoming apparent, there is no doubt that more regulations will include a clause that requires all regulated organizations to establish some form of BCM arrangement. Such a heightened appreciation of BCM at the national level can act as an impetus on the organization's state of BCM development. Though business continuity regulations may not be relevant in every industry, it is always beneficial for organizations to adopt basic BCM principles as a form of good business management.

For organizations that operate in regulated industries, it is mandatory to adhere to the regulations in order to do business. Certain cross-border legislations apply to some industries regardless of the country of operation. It is the responsibility of organizations to determine which regulations are relevant in their business activities. From the management perspective, there are benefits to incorporating regulatory requirements during the development stage of the BCMS. They help to establish business continuity as an integral part of executive management's planning instrument and position the subject as a governing process that underpins management capability during an incident.

TABLE 3.2 Stakeholder matrix table

Stakeholders	Involvement in BCMS	Characteristics			
		Interest	Control	Position	Impact on BCMS
Staff	Their continual support ensures the successful implementation and management of the BCMS	High	High	Supportive	High
Customers and shareholders	The requirements of those who depend on the organization's products and services, and those who have vested interest in its corporate performance, should be incorporated in the BCMS	High	High	Supportive	High

(Continued)

TABLE 3.2 (Continued)

| Stakeholders | Involvement in BCMS | Characteristics | | | | |
		Interest	Control	Position	Impact on BCMS
Other organizations					
• Competitors	It may be necessary to establish mutual business continuity arrangements during an incident and understand how the industry responds to incidents of a systemic nature	Low	Low	Opposed/Supportive	Medium-Low
• Suppliers	They form an essential part of the delivery system. It is important to assess the organization's third-party resilience capabilities and incorporate key suppliers, business continuity arrangements into the BCMS	Medium	High-Medium	Supportive	High-Medium
• Client organizations	The requirements include contractual, regulatory and key supply chain issues	High	High	Supportive	High
Media and press	Their inputs into the crisis communication strategies can underpin stakeholder engagements and build confidence	Low	Medium-Low	Neutral	Medium-Low
Government	Introduces national business continuity guidelines and advocates the importance of corporate preparedness	High	High	Supportive	High

FIGURE 3.2 BCMS conversion of internal and external influences into corporate advantages

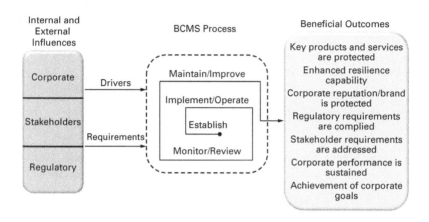

Figure 3.2 illustrates the BCMS conversion of corporate drivers, stakeholder and regulatory requirements into corporate advantages.

The following table (Table 3.3) summarizes the various techniques and tools for undertaking the activities in the organizational context analysis. These proposed techniques and tools are not an exhaustive list; rather, they suggest some useful approaches that the BCM team can adopt when undertaking this stage of the BCMS.

The internal and external drivers identified in the organizational context analysis have direct impact on the organization's ability to achieve the expected outcomes of the BCMS. As such, these drivers and their implications should form an essential part of consideration when determining the scope of the BCMS.

Organizational BCMS scoping

The purpose of BCMS scoping is to define the boundary in which the BCMS will operate. To embark on an organization-wide BCMS implementation at the outset can be an ambitious aspiration, which can often result in exhaustion of time and resources. To put it succinctly, if the project is loosely defined, it will not achieve the intended purpose of the BCMS. Likewise, a tightly defined scope may fail to include the wider business issues of the organization's operating systems, that is, the subsystems.

TABLE 3.3 Techniques and tools for undertaking organizational context analysis

Components	Activities	Techniques/Tools
Corporate Analysis	• Corporate goals, objectives and policies • Processes and resources	• Corporate documentary review • Functional audit • Process audit • Business process analysis • Organizational charts • Strategic business plans • Face-to-face interviews • Process mapping • High-level workshops
Threat and Resilience Assessment	• Identify threats and impacts • Assess corporate preparedness	• Political, economic, social and technological (PEST) analysis • Strengths, weaknesses, opportunities and threats (SWOT) analysis • Corporate documentary review • If ... then analysis • Quantitative analysis • Scenario analysis • Corporate risk register • Risk assessment
Stakeholder and Regulatory Analysis	• Stakeholders • Regulatory compliance	• Stakeholder analysis • Market trends • Workshops and seminars • Forums • Newsletters, notice boards and memoranda

The most effective approach is to incorporate the BCMS in critical areas of business and eventually expand to other parts of the organization. Such an incremental development establishes a foothold for business continuity in organizational activities. More important, it demonstrates to executive management that business continuity adds value to key processes by minimizing downtime.

To ensure that this process is conducted successfully, it is useful to note the following principles when undertaking a scoping analysis:

- The decision to include particular areas of business or building locations in the BCMS should be based on an objective review of the corporate requirements.

- The inclusion should be made in accordance to the criticality of the business and its impacts during incidents.

- As part of the scoping activity, a high-level business impact analysis (BIA) should be adopted to validate the corporate choice of the initial scope.

- An input-output process view should be adopted to consider the entire network of activities that support the delivery of key products and services.

- All relevant stakeholder and regulatory requirements, together with their implications, should be taken into consideration when making the decision on the scope of the BCMS.

- The duration of the BCMS project should be based on its extent and complexity, as determined by the scoping analysis.

- All outsourced functions or processes that are part of the organization's delivery system should be included in the scoping analysis.

- The organization should document the scope of its BCMS.

- Those areas of business excluded from the BCMS should have some forms of risk management arrangements in place. If no actions are adopted, reasons for that decision should be documented.

A good starting place for BCMS scoping is at the board level. It is much easier to conduct the analysis as part of the organization's long-range planning where key management decisions can readily be made. A functional scoping analysis can be used to identify critical and critical-supporting functions, as well as to understand their role in supporting the delivery of the organization's products and services.

The purpose of this approach is to determine which areas contribute to the fulfilment of corporate objectives and obligations. All processes, particularly those that form part of the critical supply network, should be included in the BCMS. This proposed technique is adaptable and can be adopted in organizations operating in public or private sectors, regardless of the type, size and nature of business. The extent of the scoping activity is largely dependent on the time and resources the organization is willing to commit.

The functional scoping analysis is a three-stage process:

1 Define and agree on the terms 'critical', 'critical-supporting' and 'supporting' functions

2 Identify organizational functions and processes

3 Establish the relationship and interaction between functions

Define and agree on the terms 'critical', 'critical-supporting' and 'supporting' functions

The activity should involve directors and their representatives of major functions within the organization. It is important for those who participate in this process to possess a substantial working knowledge of their functional activities. The aim of this exercise is to define and agree on what constitute 'critical', 'critical-supporting' and 'supporting' functions in the organization. The central focus is on the critical and critical-supporting functions, which should fall in the BCMS coverage.

In many cases when defining these terms, debates on their meanings arise. It is a common scenario that all who are present consider their functions 'critical' or 'critical-supporting'. However, the object of the activity is to develop an understanding of what is essential to support the organization's objectives and obligations.

The following are some questions that can act as a basis for discussion:

1 What are the organization's key objectives and obligations?

2 How are the objectives and obligations going to be achieved?

3 What outputs are required to meet the objectives and obligations?

4 What functions and critical processes are required to deliver the outputs?

5 When do the objectives and obligations need to be achieved?

Most organizations should have their own terms and classification criteria for defining critical functions. This should not be an onerous task, but, for the benefit of readers, this book suggests the following definitions and concepts that can be adapted:

- Critical functions – These functions are directly responsible for the delivery of products and services; it is the delivery of these outputs that enables the organization to fulfil its corporate objectives and obligations.

- Critical-supporting functions – The critical functions require the 'outputs' of critical-supporting functions in order to operate. They are considered as the single points of failure if they are the only sources of supply to the critical functions.

- Supporting functions – These functions provide support to the critical and critical-supporting functions by enabling them to focus on their primary activities. Their failure during an incident does not compromise the organization's ability to fulfil its objectives and obligations.

Identify organizational functions and processes

The participants involved in this activity should adequately represent the major functions in the organization. Equally important, they should recapitulate the business expectations and consider how their respective functions contribute to the delivery process to meet these aspirations.

Establish the relationship and interaction between functions

This stage calls for an objective assessment of the functional activities that support the delivery of the organization's key products and services. The following diagram (Figure 3.3) provides the functional overview of a food and beverage organization. For illustration, in this case the corporate goal is *to be the leading producer of quality beverage products in the market, bolstered by research and technologies.*

FIGURE 3.3 Relationships and interactions between functions

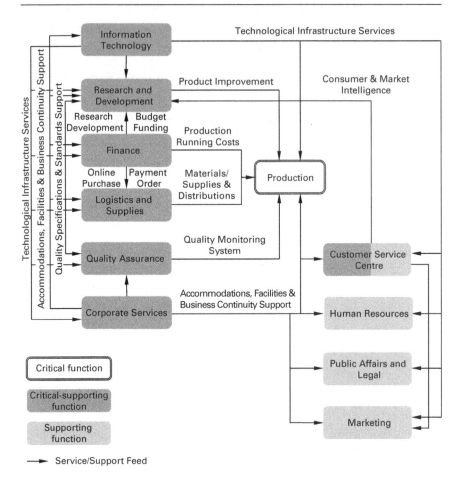

Production is considered to be the critical function since it is responsible for the final delivery of the organization's beverage products. Though there is a network of intricate relationships and interactions between functions, some functions are considered supplementary; that is, they do not form the core group that contributes directly to the finished products. Their role is to support other functions in their focus on primary activities. These supporting functions include the Consumer Service Centre (there is a critical-supporting unit in the function), Human Resources, Public Affairs and Legal, and Marketing.

In brief, the role of the Consumer Service Centre is to address consumer feedback about the organization's products and to liaise with Marketing, which is tasked with the responsibility of developing strategies to raise consumer awareness of the corporate products in different markets. However, there is a critical-supporting service in the Consumer Service Centre that provides consumer and market intelligence to Research and Development on how the existing products can be improved. In contrast, specific activities such as recruitment, training, and talent management (Human Resources) and contractual business arrangements and other legal matters (Public Affairs and Legal) do not affect the operation of critical-supporting functions.

Corporate Services and Information Technology are the functions that provide a range of physical and technological infrastructure services to all other functions. They are mutually reliant and are independent sources of supply to various functions. They do not require the support of other functions to operate. Predominantly, Corporate Services is responsible for managing all accommodation and facilities requirements. The function also has a critical role in the organization's BCM programme, particularly in the area of workplace recovery.

On the other hand, technological infrastructures managed by Information Technology establish an organization-wide system that connects all functions into a single entity of operation. Computing provides support in the forms of customized software packages, storage and production systems that enable organizational activities to be carried out more efficiently. In the event of an incident, the business recovery process would require the collaborative efforts of the two functions. As such, a thorough assessment of the processes and dependencies of these critical-supporting functions should be conducted. This includes third-party arrangements, specialist vendors and critical infrastructure providers (telecommunications and power supply). Together with Research and Development, Finance, Logistics and Supplies, and Quality Assurance, they form the critical-supporting functions. These functions provide key supports to the critical function and should therefore fall within the scope of the BCMS.

For instance, online payment (Finance) is directly linked to the inventory system (Logistics and Supplies), which provides information to the product manufacturing process (Production). The quality of these products is managed by Quality Assurance, which adopts a customized system to control outputs at various stages of the production process. These requirements are established in accordance to the specifications developed by Research and Development.

Although this proposed technique is useful to understand how key functions work as a whole and can inform the scope of the BCMS, care must be taken to ensure that the process does not lead to an oversimplified analysis because organizations operate in different models and vary in terms of risk appetites, management strategies and outsourcing arrangements. Though the above case illustrates the process of functional scoping, the concepts can be adapted to identify other aspects of the organization's operations, such as critical work locations. Once the scope has been confirmed, the next stage involves a more detailed analytical review to evaluate the criticality of the critical and critical-supporting functions based on a range of threats to and impacts on the organization (see Chapter 7).

Outsourced functions and services

Many organizations have recognized outsourcing services as an approach that can optimize their business agility and reduce operating costs. The decision to outsource secondary functions to affiliated organizations or external suppliers, whilst focusing on the primary activities, may be a shrewd business decision; however, it should always be justified by a sound risk assessment. Organizations need to recognize that, though the responsibility of delivering parts of business may rest on the supplier organizations, the bulk of contractual and regulatory obligations will always remain with the host organization. From the business resilience standpoint, it is important that outsourced functions are taken into account when undertaking the scoping activity. This develops a holistic perspective of the interdependencies between processes and establishes a thorough assessment of potential vulnerabilities in the delivery system.

Summary

Understanding the organizational context is the cornerstone of developing a fit-for-purpose BCMS. The central theme of this stage focuses on those internal and external drivers that are relevant to the organization. By understanding the key drivers and their implications that can influence organizational activities, the executive management team will be able to relate these issues when defining the scope for the BCMS. In addition, because of the varied nature of corporate goals, business priorities and risk appetites, it is up to individual organizations to determine what is critical to their business. There are a range of analytical tools and techniques available to support a rigorous process of analyzing the organizational context and scoping the BCMS. However, once the scope has been determined, further assessments need to be conducted to validate the choice of coverage.

CHECKLIST

This checklist is intended to support the business continuity management system (BCMS) development process	Yes	No	Action required
Has the organization completed a strategic analysis of its BCM requirements?	❑	❑	❑
Has the organization undertaken a formal threat and risk assessment of its critical processes?	❑	❑	❑
Have all stakeholders and regulatory requirements been identified and considered?	❑	❑	❑
Has the organization established a methodology of undertaking the BCMS scoping activity?	❑	❑	❑
Have the BCM implications of outsourcing functions and services been considered in the BCMS scoping activity?	❑	❑	❑

Further reading

Business Continuity Institute (2013) *Good Practice Guidelines: A guide to global good practice in business continuity*, Business Continuity Institute, Caversham

Disaster Recovery Institute International (DRII) (2012) *Professional Practices for Business Continuity Practitioners*, DRII, New York

ISO 22301:2012 – Societal security – Business continuity management systems – Requirements

ISO 22313:2012 – Societal security – Business continuity management systems – Guidance

Leadership

04

OVERVIEW

- This chapter underlines the importance of management commitment and describes the management influences that can affect the establishment of the BCMS.

- Next, the chapter explains the key role of a business continuity champion and the essential attributes.

- It introduces the business continuity policy that sets out how the BCMS should be managed and explains its development process.

- It illustrates a generic business continuity oversight structure to support the policy development framework.

- Finally, the chapter outlines the content of the business continuity policy and explains the individual items in the oversight document.

Background

One of the leading management challenges in the establishment of the BCMS is gaining board-level support. Like any major projects that could influence the way an organization operates, business continuity needs to be perceived as a management activity that adds value to business. The project itself requires the attention of the senior leadership team, also known as top management, in order to receive the correct emphasis. As defined by ISO 22301: Societal Security – Business Continuity Management Systems – Requirements, top management comprise a team of individuals at the highest level of corporate management who direct and control an organization. They hold specific executive powers conferred on them by the authority of the board of directors and key shareholders. As such, board-level commitment is paramount to success.

To ensure that the BCMS is embedded as an integral part of the organization's mainstream activities, executive leadership is essential at every stage of the project. In many organizations it is becoming a corporate norm to appoint a business continuity champion, also known as a project sponsor, to oversee the project development process. The individual is a member of the senior leadership team who provides advice to the BCM team in setting up a management-driven BCMS. This individual acts as a messenger, who conveys management resolutions to the BCM team whilst acting on behalf of the business continuity steering committee to report the status of the BCMS project and other management issues to the board. There are a number of factors that should be taken into account when establishing the role and authority of a business continuity champion.

Equally important is the business continuity policy, which reflects executive management's support for the BCMS. It defines the corporate expectation that the organization places on the BCMS. This is supported by a set of objectives stating the outcomes that the management system seeks to achieve. This high-level document provides the framework for implementing and managing the BCMS, that is, establishing the business continuity capability. A set of good practice principles to which the organization aspires and against which its BCMS performance can be assessed can also be included.

Management commitment

Depending on the size and sector in which the organization operates, internal and external drivers can influence the level of support for business continuity. These drivers can also have an impact on executive management's decision to implement the BCMS. Chief amongst these drivers are corporate governance, customer requirements and regulatory compliance, which dictate how the organizational activities are controlled and managed.

Business continuity forms an essential part of an organization's overall approach to governance. It should be treated as an executive, management-driven process. Board-level leadership, priority and budgetary support are recognized as critical factors to the successful establishment of the BCMS. These factors ensure that the management system is adequately resourced and managed. The 'top-down' approach enforces the importance of BCM across the organization, which can reduce resistance within the organizational structure. Also, it creates a positive business continuity culture, which helps to foster the integration of BCM as part of the organization's strategic and day-to-day management ethos.

At the outset, the BCMS project should be steered by a senior management figure known as the business continuity champion. This individual reports directly to the chief executive and other senior members of the executive management board, which collectively approve the necessary resources for the project.

There are several management influences that are essential for the establishment of an effective BCMS:

- Corporate alignment
- Process integration
- Staff appointment and resource planning
- Communication and compliance
- Support and empowerment
- Ongoing commitment

Corporate alignment

Executive management should take into account the strategic direction, governance and operating environment of the organization during the development of business continuity objectives and policy. Key decisions pertaining to the corporate status of the BCMS will have to be made at board level since its implications can affect how organizational activities are managed. To ensure that the BCMS becomes an integral part of organizational activities, executive management should incorporate the principles of business continuity into the strategic planning process. Such integration also helps to position business continuity as a key enabler that supports business performance and growth.

Process integration

In the broadest sense, business continuity can be integrated at two levels of organizational activities, namely, management and operations. The former focuses on the high-level positioning of BCM to safeguard strategic assets, such as reputation and shareholder value. This form of integration also improves the quality of planning, which enables the corporate strategies to be implemented with greater certainty. In contrast, the latter applies the BCMS to critical processes by developing resilience strategies to optimize product and service availability.

Staff appointment and resource planning

The success of the BCMS project requires the early appointment of key individuals and allocation of resources. It is important that executive management nominate a business continuity champion to provide oversight of the project. Predominantly, the business continuity champion acts on behalf of the board to approve proposals developed by the business continuity manager, such as the formation of the BCM team, staff roles and responsibilities, and acquisition of physical and technological resources.

Communication and compliance

Once the business continuity policy has been approved, executive management, through the business continuity champion, communicates the importance of complying with these corporate guidelines to all who are involved in the management of the BCMS. This helps to foster a collective commitment to achieve its intended outcomes.

Support and empowerment

Visible board-level backing in the form of a statement of intent signed by the chief executive, coupled with the business continuity champion's influence, can readily pave the way for a successful implementation of the BCMS. In addition, the business continuity champion should empower key individuals in the BCM team to make decisions in order that tasks can be carried out more effectively.

Ongoing commitment

The ongoing commitment from executive management helps to embed a positive business continuity culture within the organization. Such commitment can take the form of management review on how the BCMS can remain relevant to new corporate challenges. In most cases, this requires a dedicated budget for the ongoing improvement of the BCMS. Also, regular awareness programmes can heighten the profile of BCM, which helps to maintain staff support for achieving its objectives.

Business continuity champion

To ensure effective implementation of the BCMS, it is crucial to appoint a business continuity champion, whose role is to provide oversight for the project. This individual should be a senior figure representing the leadership team who can add credibility to the project. In order to demonstrate board-level support to the BCMS, it is vital that this role is formally endorsed and has visibility within the organization. Given the business continuity champion's special role in the successful establishment of the BCMS, some form of briefing would be necessary to help the individual understand the management value of business continuity.

Being a senior member of the board, the business continuity champion is involved in the formulation of the business continuity policy and objectives. This individual should have enough organizational influence to help the BCM team overcome organizational obstacles and the ability to galvanize the corporate commitment to meet the objectives set out in the business continuity policy. From the business continuity standpoint, this is particularly important when implementing the BCMS for the first time since the successful outcome of the project requires cooperative effort across the organization.

The responsibilities and authority of a business continuity champion should be commensurate with the complexity of the project. The following proposes the generic attributes of a business continuity champion:

- Business continuity awareness
- Corporate knowledge
- Organizational influence
- Budget and resource management
- Business alignment

Business continuity awareness

Preferably, the business continuity champion should be someone who can appreciate the value of business continuity in contributing to good governance. In most cases, a high-level desktop discussion or briefing about the subject can help to identify the appropriate individual. This will also enable the individual to translate board-level requirements into BCM expectations. One of the key roles of the business continuity champion is to raise awareness of business continuity at board level, which helps to promote the subject as a strategic planning tool.

Corporate knowledge

A business continuity champion represents the executive management perspective in setting up the expectation for BCM. In this sense, the individual is instrumental in shaping the position of the BCMS to support corporate goals and performance. In order to do this, the individual is required to have a clear understanding of the objectives, strategies and risk appetite so that the relationship between organizational requirements and business continuity can be established.

Organizational influence

The business continuity champion should be visible throughout the organization reflecting management leadership in the BCMS project. The individual acts as an advocate for the project to enable all involved to get work done without serious antagonism. This includes protecting the project from management politics as well as fencing the necessary resources in order that they are not assigned for the benefit of another. During the implementation stage, the individual provides advisory oversight to the business continuity manager by emphasizing the importance of adhering to the project vision and guidelines.

Budget and resource management

Since most resources need to be approved at the highest level, the business continuity champion is generally seen as the leading figure in obtaining the key resources, such as budget and the appointment of a business continuity manager. The individual can also be responsible for ensuring that the project is managed within the approved budget and may be required to secure additional resources; in most cases, though, the task of project management is delegated to the business continuity manager.

Business alignment

In an effort to position BCM as a corporate planning tool, the business continuity champion needs to advocate the importance of business continuity to the board when making strategic decisions. This helps the senior leadership team to align the BCMS with the long-term direction of the organization. At the project level, the individual directs the implementation team to integrate the BCM activities into the organization's critical activities.

Business continuity policy

The business continuity policy sets out how the BCMS should be managed in an agreed and controlled manner. Like other major policies, an integral part of the business continuity policy contains a statement underlining the importance the organization places on BCM.

It is important to note that the policy document is the ownership of executive management. The review of the document resides at board level. In order for the BCMS to be effectively embedded in organizational activities, the business continuity champion, together with the senior leadership team, should ensure that the policy is adequately aligned to other corporate policies and strategies.

Policy development

The stages of business continuity policy development form an important aspect of setting up the BCMS. The business continuity manager, with the support of the BCM team, proposes the development process to the business continuity champion, who will then present to the board for approval. It is worth noting that the process of policy development is not a one-time process but one that can be consultative and lengthy, depending on organizational factors such as management priority, project timescale and resource availability. The following diagram illustrates the basic stages of the policy development framework (Figure 4.1).

Formation of working groups/teams

The first stage focuses on the identification of key individuals and BCM working groups to support the policy development framework. Broadly, two groups of staff are involved in the development process. The first group comprises members of the senior leadership team who make strategic decisions about the organization and its resources. In contrast, the second group consists of specialist staff with technical knowledge about BCM.

FIGURE 4.1 Policy development framework

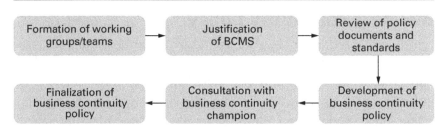

- Appoint a business continuity champion.

- Appoint a business continuity manager (note: depending on organizational circumstances, the business continuity manager can be nominated prior to the appointment of the business continuity champion).

- Have the business continuity manager define the working structure, such as teams and modes of communication, and propose them to the business continuity champion.

- Define membership criteria for working committees, teams and individuals. It is important to consider their roles and impact on the BCMS. Additional requirements for individuals include knowledge, skills and competencies.

- Discuss particular business issues pertaining to business continuity through business fora and working groups. Representatives from various functions are nominated to provide collective views to the business continuity steering committee.

Figure 4.2 illustrates a generic business continuity oversight structure.

Justification of BCMS

This stage defines the purpose of the BCMS. In most cases, a review of documents related to corporate governance can identify performance gaps in organizational resilience and be used as a basis to establish a case for business continuity.

- Gather and review recent national and international incidents with adverse impacts.

- Relate those cases that are relevant to the organization.

- Use desktop discussions with key parties to review the organization's current resilience strategies and preparedness. Equally important, the organization's critical suppliers should form part of the discussion.

- Identify stakeholder and regulatory requirements that are relevant to the organization.

FIGURE 4.2 Business continuity oversight structure

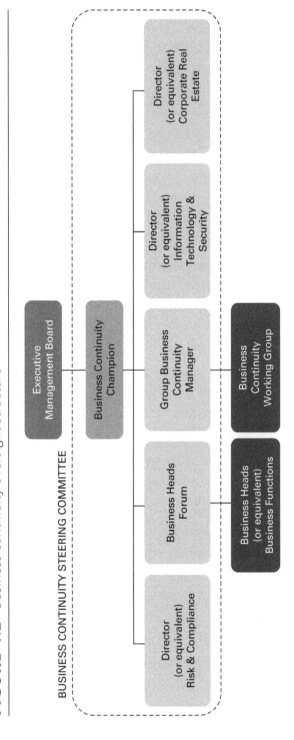

BUSINESS CONTINUITY STEERING COMMITTEE

Executive Management Board

Business Continuity Champion

Director (or equivalent) Risk & Compliance

Business Heads Forum

Group Business Continuity Manager

Director (or equivalent) Information Technology & Security

Director (or equivalent) Corporate Real Estate

Business Heads (or equivalent) Business Functions

Business Continuity Working Group

- Address management practices that are not aligned with internal and external requirements. Audit findings are useful evidence to support the case for business continuity.

Review of policy documents and standards

The review stage focuses on the assessment of the organization's business continuity policy against professional guidelines or policies of other organizations operating in the same or related industries (if they are available).

- Identify good practice guidelines published by professional or standards bodies and review against the organization's business continuity policy.
- Perform a benchmarking study or a gap analysis of the organization's current business continuity policy against principles of other 'better' policies.
- Identify and incorporate good practice elements into the organization's business continuity policy.
- If necessary, seek advice from industry regulators or business continuity professional bodies.

Development of business continuity policy

In most cases, the BCM team is tasked with the development of the business continuity policy template. This stage includes the identification of key information resources for the policy.

- Define key items of the business continuity policy.
- Draft the policy template or adapt a 'good practice' policy template according to the organizational context.
- Incorporate pertinent information from relevant sources, such as BCM and risk-related policies, high-level scoping analysis and audits. This ensures that the business continuity policy is aligned to address the management issues.
- Seek comments from key individuals who have intimate knowledge about the organization such as corporate goals, strategies, and critical products and services.

- Ensure the business continuity policy is aligned with other related policies, such as risk, security, and health and safety.

Consultation with business continuity champion

The completed draft business continuity policy is presented to the business continuity champion and executive management team. The purpose of this stage is to gain the team's participation in the business continuity policy-making process.

- Have the business continuity manager present and circulate the draft policy to the business continuity champion and the board for consultation.
- Collate feedback from the group and amend the draft policy.

Finalization of business continuity policy

The final stage of the process is to obtain executive endorsement of the business continuity policy. Once approved, the policy document is disseminated to the wider groups within the organization.

- Obtain the business continuity champion's approval of the revised policy.
- Have the business continuity champion, with the support of the business continuity manager, seek executive approval and sign-off of the business continuity policy.
- Publish and disseminate the business continuity policy using the organization's document control system.
- Ensure that the implementation framework of the BCMS has been agreed upon by executive management.
- Implement the agreed framework to kick-start the BCMS setting-up activities.

The above process is intended to provide a simplified overview of the key stages in the development of a business continuity policy – from the appointment of a business continuity champion leading to a full-fledged business continuity policy. Depending on the state of an organization's BCM maturity, it may be necessary to implement the stages in parallel during the development of the policy.

Business continuity policy content

The business continuity policy is a formal document that describes the key aspects of the organization's BCMS. In essence, the items of a business continuity policy include or make reference to the following:

- Statement of endorsement
- BCMS scope
- Business continuity objectives
- BCMS lifecycle
- Review period
- Roles and responsibilities
- Structure and membership
- Communication
- Assumptions and limitations
- References

Statement of endorsement

The policy should reflect the commitment of executive management to the BCMS. This is generally in a formal statement endorsed by a senior figure of the senior leadership team, preferably the chief executive or equivalent. It comprises the corporate definition of business continuity and how the management process is applied in the organization.

BCMS scope

This can be based on the outcome of a BCMS scoping analysis or an informed decision made at board level. In essence, the scope of implementation sets out three areas of focus: breadth, depth and corporate resources. Breadth informs the coverage of the BCMS whilst depth describes the defined level of preparedness, that is, the extent of planning activities. Corporate resources refer to the types of organizational assets required to implement the BCMS.

Business continuity objectives

Broadly, business continuity objectives take the form of targets to enhance organizational resilience. They should reflect the BCMS as a tool that can provide greater confidence and assurance to key products and services. When defining the business continuity objectives, it is important to take into account the stakeholder and regulatory drivers and their implications. In order to evaluate what has been achieved, or how effective the BCMS performance is, the objectives should be realistic and measureable.

BCMS lifecycle

The BCMS lifecycle is the framework that outlines the different stages of establishing the BCMS. Each stage illustrates a series of processes that must be carried out, with the associated deliverables. It is useful to incorporate good practice guidelines and standards into the BCMS lifecycle. This ensures that the organization's BCMS is established based on sound principles and has considered the latest issues in the business continuity industry.

Review period

The purpose of the review period is to provide the planned intervals in which the review of the BCMS will take place. It ensures that the BCMS processes remain adequate and responsive to changes in organizational requirements. This is an opportunity to identify areas of improvement in the BCMS, including the reassessment of the business continuity policy and objectives.

Roles and responsibilities

A key item of the business continuity policy is the appointment of key individuals to manage the BCMS. This ensures that roles and responsibilities are assigned to appropriate individuals, who are empowered to accomplish the tasks. An effective approach is to adopt the RACI matrix:

- Responsible – Individuals are assigned with the responsibilities for getting the tasks complete. The individuals are given the autonomy to make decisions within the scope of their work.

- Accountable – Individuals are usually the leading figures who are accountable for the entire project. The individuals ensure that tasks are completed to the required specifications and approve their completion.

- Consulted – Individuals are provided with pertinent information to make decisions relating to the project.

- Informed – Individuals are kept informed about the status of the project. They have a vested interest in the project.

Structure and membership

The policy should define the qualifications for the BCM structure. The management structure refers to working groups, committees and teams that are responsible for managing the BCMS, whilst qualifications provide the criteria for membership and remit of individual groupings. In essence, there are two forms of structure, namely, business-as-usual (BAU) and management of business continuity (MBC). The BAU structure assumes the management of the BCMS: from the development to improvement of the business continuity capability. In contrast, the MBC structure, also known as the incident management structure, deals with the actual management of an incident, which involves collaboration between local incident management teams and the central BCM team. Depending upon the size and diversity of the organization, the management structure could range from a simple working team to a complex structure of multilayered committees supported by subgroups.

Communication

The business continuity policy should set out the communication strategies to key individuals and groups. It generally outlines what business continuity information needs to be communicated and covers the methods of communication. The purpose is to raise the importance of good BCM, whilst enforcing conformity to the BCMS requirements. In addition, there should be a document control system that describes the procedures in terms of the distribution, access, retrieval and use of business continuity materials.

Assumptions and limitations

The initial setting up of the BCMS often calls for a set of planning assumptions to enable the planning team to design the management system with greater certainty. However, there are limits to such an approach: deviations can occur as the reality unfolds, which can readily compromise the integrity of the entire BCMS. As such, the policy needs to state the assumptions on which the corporate business continuity capability is based and set out the limitations of the BCMS.

References

The reference section highlights the relevant BCM standards that the organization aspires to achieve. It should provide a summary description of the standards and justifications for their adoption. In addition, it should include the relationship between the BCMS and the corporate governance, and indicate where further information can be obtained.

Summary

An effective BCMS is about aligning its requirements to support the organization's goals and strategies. This entails the creation of a setting within which the management system can readily be embedded in key organizational activities and be recognized as a mainstream management discipline. Essentially, this calls for management leadership, which is often represented by a senior member of staff, known as the business continuity champion. Equally important is the business continuity policy, which outlines board-level commitment and the value the organization places on the BCMS. This high-level document provides a blueprint for the establishment of the corporate business continuity capability to deal with uncertainties. In order to develop and maintain confidence in the BCMS, ongoing commitment throughout the organization is essential.

CHECKLIST

This checklist is intended to support the business continuity management system (BCMS) development process	Yes	No	Action required
Is the BCMS fully endorsed and driven by the senior leadership team?	☐	☐	☐
Is a member of the senior leadership team assigned overall accountability for the implementation of the BCMS?	☐	☐	☐
Have the management influences that could impact the implementation of the BCMS been identified?	☐	☐	☐
Is there a defined business continuity oversight structure to provide supervision of the policy development process?	☐	☐	☐
Does the organization have a clearly defined, documented and approved business continuity policy?	☐	☐	☐
Have the BCMS requirements been clearly defined and documented in the business continuity policy?	☐	☐	☐

References

ISO 22301:2012 – Societal security – Business continuity management
   systems – Requirements

Further reading

Business Continuity Institute (2013) *Good Practice Guidelines: A guide to global good practice in business continuity*, Business Continuity Institute, Caversham

Disaster Recovery Institute International (DRII) (2012) Professional Practices for Business Continuity Practitioners, DRII, New York

ISO 22313:2012 – Societal security – Business continuity management systems – Guidance

Planning

05

OVERVIEW

- This chapter first explains the two main approaches to corporate resilience and examines the key strategies for controlling risks.
- It goes on to explain the importance of business continuity objectives and highlights the three forms of objectives that are commonly defined in the BCMS.
- Next, it introduces the generic process of developing business continuity objectives.
- This chapter then provides a sample list of objectives and their attributes of measurement.
- Finally, it explains the project management process for initiating the BCMS.

Background

The increasing volatility of the business environment has exposed organizations to a myriad of influences, notably, economic uncertainties, competition, stringent requirements, and natural and human-induced threats. This presents challenges to the senior leadership team; some challenges offer opportunities whilst others are risks that could impede performance if they are not adequately managed. As such, management executives should consider a range of risk mitigation strategies to address potential threats to organizational activities. The object is to minimize the risks by establishing organizational controls whilst maximizing the potential opportunities to further growth. Doing so demonstrates to the stakeholders that the organization has an established resilience programme, which proactively safeguards the delivery of critical products and services in order to fulfil its objectives and statutory obligations.

When considering a strategy, or combination of strategies, to control the undesired effects of risks to the organization, it is important to discern whether they are able to meet the intended outcomes specified in the business continuity policy. In most cases, the outcomes are in the form of objectives that provide guiding statements of what actions should be directed. The objectives form the basis in shaping the nature of the BCMS, that is, the approach in which the business continuity capability is developed to support the corporate goals. Therefore, due consideration should be given to the development of objectives and how the desired outcomes will be measured. Building a BCMS is much like any other business project. It first requires the development of a project plan – a formal project management process that outlines the main activities, individuals, resources and critical success factors that are essential to an effective BCMS.

Approaches to corporate resilience

Broadly, there are two approaches to corporate resilience: the management approach and the process-centric approach. The management approach places emphasis on compliance, corporate defences and corporate structure in the organization. In contrast, the process-centric approach is activity-orientated; it addresses threats to the core business operations with actions to minimize their likelihood and impact. The two approaches are not mutually exclusive; joining the methods will provide an all-encompassing framework that minimizes the likelihood of critical products and services being affected by an incident.

Management approach

The management approach is about building resilience throughout the organization at all levels. It focuses on the 'soft' issues of staff behaviours and actions. Most of the measures are directed towards prevention with the principle of reducing the probability of an incident. The following are examples of management approaches:

- Compliance
- Corporate defences
- Corporate structure

Compliance

In general, compliance falls into two types of mandatory requirements, namely, internal and external. Internal requirements are actions that must be taken by staff to comply with the corporate governance and other key policies. On the other hand, external requirements are imposed by the wider environment, that is, the industry and the country in which the organization operates. From the business continuity standpoint, the purpose of compliance is to assure stakeholders that organizational activities and risks are adequately managed. The organization should maintain a set of procedures to determine the legal and regulatory requirements that are pertinent to its corporate activities. These requirements should be reviewed regularly in the corporate governance and policies. It is also important that reviews are undertaken at planned intervals to assess the extent compliance has been met.

Corporate defences

Corporate defences include guidelines, procedures and physical control systems. Guidelines and procedures are useful means to ensure staff adhere to the organization's standard of practice. They establish controls to regulate the organizational environment and detect warning signals before they become an incident. This often calls for the development of effective communication protocols for reporting near-misses and corporate breaches. In contrast, physical control systems help to protect the organization's assets and provide security to facilities, premises and information technology. They are generally considered as risk-reduction measures. Though they offer some level of prevention, their primary function is to limit the impact and losses to the organization. The controls can be classified as active and passive.

Active controls include manned closed circuit camera surveillance and mobile security staff whilst passive controls include firewalls, passwords, sprinkler system and backup generators.

Corporate structure

The corporate structure outlines the management hierarchy of the organization. The management hierarchy establishes reporting lines of communication, which in turn influence how the organization is managed. The corporate structure determines how quickly and efficiently early warning signals are transmitted across the organization. It is not surprising that a structure based on a rigid bureaucratic system has the propensity to incubate an organizational crisis. In many cases, the information that needs to get to the relevant people could be either distorted or delayed. In short, the structure is influenced by the corporate procedures established by the senior leadership team, which can either facilitate or inhibit open communication.

Process-centric approach

The process-centric approach adopts the discipline of risk management to safeguard the organization's critical processes. This approach consists of six types of strategies:

- Modification
- Reduction
- Transfer
- Retention and loss mitigation controls
- Insurance
- Business continuity management

Modification

Once the risks have been identified and assessed, it may be necessary to change the methods of production or undertake minor modifications to the activities, whilst making little impact on the cost and duration of the delivery. By changing certain features of the delivery activities, it may be possible to reduce the number or concentration of risks. However, making such a decision requires a thorough evaluation of the entire production system. It is important to ensure that corporate performance is not compromised by such changes. This option is often adopted where the product or service has a limited lifespan.

Reduction

Risk reduction falls into three basic categories. First, awareness and training programmes that alert staff to potential risks and the possible mitigation measures. Second, physical protection that minimizes the likelihood of an incident or reduces the impact of losses. As discussed earlier, physical control systems, which can be active and passive, are typical risk-reduction measures. Third, a combination of mitigation strategies to manage risks. For instance, it may be possible to devise methods of avoiding certain risks whilst making minor changes to the delivery process.

Transfer

This option is about transferring the risk from the host organization to a third party without changing the characteristics of risk in the process. However, due care should be taken when establishing this type of arrangement. Often, the decision to transfer or allocate risk to a third party is implemented through the conditions of a contract. Prior to establishing this type of arrangement, several factors need to be taken into consideration. They include whether the party that the risk is transferred to is capable of managing or controlling the risk, and whether the third party could accept the consequences should the risk be manifested. It is supposed that the party that accepts the risk is best able to manage it. Though risk transfer can prove to be an appropriate option, it is important to note that certain obligations cannot be transferred; the host organization may still be liable to statutory penalties and suffer from losses as a result of delivery failure.

Retention and loss mitigation controls

When the organization can manage the risk or accept the consequences should the risk be realized, it might decide to retain the risk. The risk retained may be controllable or uncontrollable and is subject to the corporate risk appetite. This option is often supported by loss mitigation controls to minimize risks and their effects to key operations. In most cases, the corporate decision to adopt risk retention is after the risk has been treated. This is known as residual risk or net risk, after a range of mitigation measures to manage the primary risk have been implemented.

Insurance

This option provides a financial compensation or indemnity to the organization following a number of predetermined events. Due consideration should be taken when deciding on this option since it has a number of limitations. The insurance policy states the conditions in which the insurance covers the incident; where the incident is not an insured event, the organization would likely bear the brunt of the cost. Another key factor to consider is the cost of the premium for the risk insurance versus the cost of the consequences. Though the compensation may address the tangible losses, such as products, services and business properties, the most invaluable assets – reputation and consumer confidence – are unquantifiable in monetary terms. Under such circumstances, the financial settlement alone may not provide the risk-proof solution to address the business needs. It is also becoming a norm that insurers require those they insure to have risk and business continuity arrangements in place before they give a premium discount or improved terms to a business interruption policy. From the resilience standpoint, insurance is most appropriate when combined with other risk strategies.

Business continuity management

This is a holistic approach that establishes the corporate capability to safeguard the organization's high-value activities and key stakeholder interests during an adverse event. It implements a range of continuity strategies to ensure that critical operations can maintain an acceptable level of performance to fulfil the organizational obligations.

One of the most challenging tasks in management is to consider which options are most appropriate to managing the known risks. Each has its strengths and weaknesses, and it is up to the senior leadership team to decide if it is prepared to retain a risk or find some means of avoiding or transferring the risk. The fundamental rule is that stakeholder and regulatory issues should form the basis for evaluating the options.

Business continuity objectives

There are three reasons why objectives are crucial in the BCMS. The first reason is that they constitute the purpose of the organization's BCMS. In many cases, these objectives come in the form of requirements to address corporate issues, such as the incident management capability and statutory compliance. The second reason is they act as guidance for the BCM team in the formulation of actions to achieve the desired outcomes of the BCMS. The third reason is objectives are the basis for the evaluation of the organization's BCMS performance. They are used as indicators to assess the extent to which the requirements have been met and what further activities are necessary to enhance the BCMS.

In most cases, the business continuity objectives start out as general statements of intent that make reference to corporate expectations set by executive management. As work progresses, they are developed into specific requirements that focus on key aspects of the BCMS. It is important that the BCM team works closely with the business continuity champion to ensure that the objectives are compatible with the strategic goals and relevant to the organizational context.

In general, there are three forms of business continuity objective:

- People-orientated – These objectives are about shaping the attitudes, behaviours and skills of individuals or wider groups of staff that help to bring a positive change in their approach of working towards the business continuity objectives.

- Performance-orientated – These objectives focus on the BCMS performance. They are devised in accordance to management reviews that initiate continual improvement in the BCMS.

- Process-orientated – These objectives focus on the BCM activities that support the achievement of people- and performance-orientated objectives.

More often than not, business continuity objectives will fall into all three categories. These objectives can also be used as intermediate indicators to monitor the organization's BCMS progress against its defined level of performance.

Business continuity objective development

Listing objectives can be an onerous task if individuals do not have a clear concept of what an objective is. Objectives are specific measurable results that cover short- and long-term requirements of the BCMS. They stipulate the extent to which the corporate business continuity capability will be accomplished by a defined deadline.

When developing business continuity objectives, a key consideration to note is that if they do not add value to the organization's overall objectives or if they cannot be evaluated, they should not become a requirement in the business continuity policy.

Three principles should be noted when developing business continuity objectives. First, the corporate goals should form the basis for the development of business continuity objectives. Second, corporate drivers and external influences should be taken into account. Third, a determination must be made on how well a given objective supports the role of the BCMS in the organizational setting.

A fit-for-purpose business continuity objective should embody the following five attributes:

- Unambiguous – The objective should be concise and unequivocal. The statement should be expressed as clearly as possible so it can be easily understood.

- Relevant – The objective should reflect the organization's current context and help to address key corporate challenges. It should also be consistent with key policies and strategies.

- Practicality – The objective should not be overly ambitious but should be achievable. The statement should be capable of realization through the existing corporate resources, whilst taking into account the organization's current constraints.

- Measurable – The objective must be capable of being assessed; that is, the information pertaining to the objective can be collated and translated into comparative terms.

- Time-based – The objective should be attainable within a given timeframe. This ensures that corporate resources are allocated to achieve the BCMS requirement by a defined deadline. It also provides an opportunity to assess progress.

It is worth noting that, as the business continuity objectives are being developed, the stages may not follow a linear sequence; some stages may run in parallel. However, for the benefit of readers who are new to the discipline, the process is presented in a sequential order. Seasoned professionals may still find the process a useful guide when conducting their annual reviews of the business continuity objectives. The stages are as follows:

- Review corporate vision and mission statements
- Collate corporate information
- Define and review issues that need to be addressed
- Analyze the gap
- Develop business continuity objectives
- Define measures for evaluation

Review corporate vision and mission statements

The review of mission statements can appropriately align the BCMS to support the organizational goals. This establishes business continuity as a mainstream activity that underpins corporate performance by ensuring adequate resilience is built into key processes.

Collate corporate information

The collection of corporate information provides evidence on the state of organizational preparedness, which can determine the performance gaps and define the areas of improvement. In the broadest sense, corporate information includes risk-related policies, audit reports, management reviews and plans.

Define and review issues that need to be addressed

This stage identifies points of weakness in critical processes and focuses on those deficiencies that can compromise the organization's delivery system. These impending issues can help to galvanize support of executive management for the BCMS project.

Analyse the gap

Another useful approach is to conduct a gap analysis. This technique is used to assess the organization's current BCMS performance against the potential level it strives to achieve. It is an effective approach to identify shortcomings in the business continuity capability. Information from the gap analysis can help to guide objectives development and actions required to move the BCMS from its present state to the desired future state.

Develop business continuity objectives

This stage focuses on what progress needs to be accomplished in the organization's business continuity capability. It is important that the business continuity objectives are realistic and take into account the organizational capacity to achieve them. This includes the availability of critical knowledge and skills, dedicated budget and resource supports. In order to secure executive support for the BCMS, the business continuity manager should develop objectives that demonstrate the value business continuity brings to optimizing the organization's productive ability.

Define measures for evaluation

Measures are directly related to the formulation of objectives. They should be direct and unambiguous. Measures should clearly reflect the characteristics of the objective they are related to in order to provide clear connection between the findings and the intended outcomes. They should be specific for the evaluation to be carried out in absolute terms.

Table 5.1 offers a sample list of objectives and their attributes of measurement grouped under the key areas of the BCMS.

TABLE 5.1 Business continuity objectives and their attributes of measurement

Business Continuity Objectives	Measures
Support	
• To gain executive commitment to BCMS	– BCM becomes part of the agenda in executive management's regular meetings
	– Annual budget dedicated to BCMS
	– Business continuity is adopted in the strategic planning process
	– Member of the senior leadership team is appointed as the business continuity champion
• To develop a formal business continuity policy that clearly defines guidance for implementing business continuity capability	– Business continuity policy contains the implementation framework for the BCMS and is endorsed by the chief executive or equivalent
	– Mission statement and objectives are clearly defined and documented in the business continuity policy
Culture	
• To enhance the skills and competencies of members in the BCM team	– Number of BCM courses attended by individual team members per year
	– Professional certification of team members
	– Achievement of business continuity competency objectives set out in staff appraisal reports
Process: Business impact analysis (BIA)	
• To define the business impacts of critical products and services	– BIA report documents details of the BIA process – the identification and documentation of critical products and services
	– Description of individual critical products and services detailing their recovery time objectives, resources and minimum levels of operation

(Continued)

TABLE 5.1 (*Continued*)

Business Continuity Objectives	Measures
Process: Threat/Risk assessment • To identify and evaluate the threats to key operations • To develop a plan of actions to address the identified threats to key business operations	– Risk assessment report contains details of the vulnerability and exposure of key operations to specific threats and risk concentrations – Risk management strategies are clearly defined and documented in the risk management plan and policy
Process: Incident response structure • To establish the incident management structure (IMS) that enables an effective response and recovery from disruptions	– Business continuity policy outlines the IMS and its requirements in terms of processes and procedures – Desktop exercise that requires the participation of all members of the IMS. This ensures that their collective effort can confirm, control and contain an incident – Protocol is established within the IMS to communicate with key stakeholders
Plans • To develop the business continuity plan (BCP) that provides effective responses to safeguard the continuity of critical products and services	– Clearly documented set of procedures for addressing key issues from the initial response to the point at which normal business operations are resumed – Procedures validated by exercises
Exercise • To assess BCM team members' familiarity of their roles and responsibilities	– Observation during the exercise – Conduct a post-exercise debrief and analysis to seek members' feedback pertaining to the challenges they encountered – Compare outcomes of the exercise with results of the last exercise

(*Continued*)

TABLE 5.1 *(Continued)*

Business Continuity Objectives	Measures
Maintenance	
• To ensure that the corporate business continuity capability remains effective, adequate and up-to-date to meet the organizational requirements	– Up-to-date BCM documents that reflect corporate changes
	– Business continuity policy, strategies and BCPs continue to be relevant to management strategies, priorities and goals
	– Exercise reports serve as documented evidence of proactive management of the corporate business continuity capability

BCMS project management

Establishing the BCMS is much like any other corporate project. A formal project management methodology is essential to plan, coordinate and manage various activities in order to successfully deliver the project outcomes. At the minimum, an effective BCMS project management should contain the following:

- Resources
- Roles and responsibilities
- BCMS tasks
- Project critical success factors
- Project risk assessment

Resources

One of the prerequisites for the successful implementation of the BCMS is the presence of a dedicated budget. Such funding is used to galvanize key resources such as staff, technological infrastructures, administrative and management tools to support the implementation of the management system. The extent of the resources required will depend upon the complexity of the BCMS.

Planning and controlling the use of resources in an effective manner is a job in its own right. For organizations operating in several regions across the country or on different continents, it can be a challenge to organize resources to implement a corporate-wide BCMS. Therefore, it makes good sense to plan for the optimal use of resources. Even where the BCMS is operated in a single-site organization, it is still necessary to take formal steps to plan and manage resources.

One effective approach to managing business continuity resources is the use of standard project scheduling software to allocate resources to individual tasks, which can provide a means for assessing the status of utilization. Also crucial in this respect is to avoid unnecessary levels of detail that serve to do little more than complicate the entire BCMS project.

Roles and responsibilities

The implementation of the organization's BCMS is a complex process that requires support from a wide range of managerial and operational roles. At this stage, it is assumed that there is a suitable business continuity manager and business continuity champion in place (otherwise the funding would not have happened) to initiate the BCMS project. Their first principal task is the design of the corporate business continuity planning structure, that is, the identification of individual roles and teams to support the project.

The assignment of roles and responsibilities is a vital element in the BCMS project since individuals involved in the development process may be called upon to manage the actual incident. For this reason, the business continuity manager should ensure that key members of the team possess the essential knowledge and skills or undergo appropriate training if necessary. In the case where the BCMS project is introduced across a number of different locations, the local project teams assume the role of implementing the BCM activities whilst the central BCM team provides the project oversight.

Figure 5.1 depicts the business continuity management structure of an international financial services organization.

FIGURE 5.1 Business continuity management structure

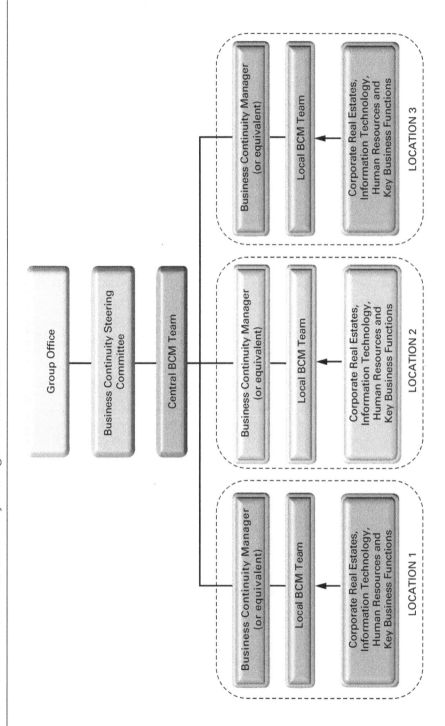

BCMS tasks

Prior to the implementation of the BCMS, the planning tasks can be subdivided, where appropriate and practical, into key stages of the business continuity lifecycle. In most cases, the BCMS project is somewhat sequential (at least from the first glance at the project plan). However, in reality many tasks run in parallel when the project is implemented. One effective approach is to select an estimated start date and end date, and allocate deadlines to individual tasks. It is also important to check if any tasks need to be resequenced because of unrealistic timescales or conflict with other tasks. In some cases, the subsequent stages are dependent on the deliverables of the preceding stages. For instance, findings from the business impact analysis and risk assessment are required for the strategy selection and development stage before business continuity solutions can be devised. The focus here is to identify to what extent the tasks can be packaged and performed.

A starting point is to write a brief description about each task accompanied with the planning assumptions. This is useful in estimating the time required for completion as well as establishing controls to ensure the work stays within its scope. At the minimum, each task should include the following details:

- Objectives – The outcomes of the task. Objectives are specific measurable results that are used to define the deliverables.
- Scope – This refers to the area of operation in which the task and its activities should be performed, which also helps to prevent any 'spill over' of task.
- Task – A description of the work and activities that need to be done. It is important that the task complies with the requirements set out by the organization's business continuity policy.
- Timescale – The timeframe for the task completion.
- Essential skills: Skill profiles for the task. It is useful to include the nominated staff responsible for the task.
- Resources – The additional resources required to perform the task, such as software packages, information, and technological and management tools.

- Communication structure – A diagram that illustrates the relationship between various parties. It can be divided into the types of involvement required from each role: responsible, accountable, consulted and informed (RACI) (see Chapter 4). This is also used for escalating issues and making decisions.

- Deliverables – These refer to specific task products or outcomes that are required in order to complete the project.

Project critical success factors

The business continuity manager should consider those factors that are critical to the project's success, also known as critical success factors (CSFs). CSFs are actions that must be performed well in order for the defined project tasks to be satisfactorily achieved. They help the project team to devise controls to mitigate effects that can prevent the project from achieving its expected outcomes. CSFs of the BCMS project include the following:

- Project endorsement from top management
- Staff commitment and cooperation throughout the project
- Clearly defined plans with assigned roles and responsibilities
- Defined project scope and focus
- Project team empowerment
- Effective communication
- Effective project management process
- A formal issue management structure

Project risk assessment

Like any projects, implementing the BCMS project brings its own set of risks. The risks faced by one business continuity manager and team are likely to be different from another since projects are influenced by a range of factors, such as corporate drivers, environmental dynamics and the competence of individuals who perform the tasks. However, most projects share the same basic risks to their success. Some common risks to the BCMS project include the following:

- The competence of the BCM team: Having a shrewd and capable business continuity manager is not sufficient to ensure the success of the project. The manager needs a group of qualified staff to support the project implementation. Low experience adds risk to the project whilst extensive experience reduces the level of risk and ensures tasks are effectively performed.

- Executive support for the BCMS project: Lack of enthusiasm from executive management could result in inadequate budgetary support for the project. The appointment of a business continuity champion coupled with quick wins (in the forms of project deliverables) could alleviate the risk.

- Multiple functions or locations: The project might not meet its objectives if multiple organizational functions or locations are involved at any one time. This could be a constraint if the BCM team does not have the adequate resources, skills and experience. If possible, initiate a separate project for each business or location and do not attempt to deal with them all as one project.

- Organizational activities: When there are a number of key activities taking place in the organization, such as an audit, the BCMS project could be relegated from the mainstream focus of management priorities. Staff with partial roles in the BCMS project are more likely to be diverted to undertake those immediate assignments at hand. This could directly impede the project flow and its overall development.

- Unrealistic deadlines: When unrealistic dates are imposed on the project, it is most likely that the tasks will either be unattainable or the quality of deliverables will be compromised. Such consequences could affect the integrity of the BCMS. This could reflect a negative image on the BCM team and their assignment. Worse, it erodes executive confidence and support for the BCMS initiative.

Summary

Evaluation of the most appropriate mitigation option is largely influenced by internal and external organizational factors. These options should be viewed as the fundamental elements of business continuity capability. The business continuity objectives are used to shape the state of the organization's BCMS. They also act as indicators to assess the extent to which the requirements have been met. When implementing the BCMS, it is important to note that successful realization of the project will depend on careful planning, continuous monitoring and controlling various CSFs.

CHECKLIST

This checklist is intended to support the business continuity management system (BCMS) development process	Yes	No	Action required
Does the organization have appropriate corporate resilience strategies to minimize the likelihood of critical products and services affected by an incident?	☐	☐	☐
Are business continuity objectives clearly defined to measure the performance of the BCMS?	☐	☐	☐
Are the attributes of measurement realistic and measurable?	☐	☐	☐
Has the organization agreed upon an approach to implement and manage the BCMS?	☐	☐	☐

Further reading

Business Continuity Institute (2013) *Good Practice Guidelines: A guide to global good practice in business continuity*, Business Continuity Institute, Caversham

Disaster Recovery Institute International (DRII) (2012) *Professional Practices for Business Continuity Practitioners*, DRII, New York

ISO 22301:2012 – Societal security – Business continuity management systems – Requirements

ISO 22313:2012 – Societal security – Business continuity management systems – Guidance

Support

06

OVERVIEW

- This chapter first outlines resource allocation in the context of the BCMS.

- It goes on to discuss the professional practices of BCM professionals and examine the skills required to manage the BCMS.

- Next, it introduces the performance appraisal of BCM staff and examines the key approaches to evaluate staff competence.

- This chapter also looks into establishing a business continuity awareness and training programme in the organization.

- From there it discusses the principles of communication during an incident and how to develop internal and external communication protocols.

- Finally, the chapter covers the essential attributes of BCMS documentation management and explains the principles of developing an effective documentation management system.

Background

At the heart of an effective BCMS is the ability to manage the organization's BCM activities. This is directly influenced by the skills of BCM staff, namely, management, leadership, communication, analysis and coordination. Due consideration should therefore be given to the continual development of staff competence.

In addition, an appropriate corporate programme should be established to galvanize organizational support for maintaining the efficacy of the BCMS. This will require the programme to be actively supported by executive and general staff through participation in various awareness and training activities.

It is important that the organization has an established incident communication structure. This entails protocols for disseminating information to external stakeholders, which may be called upon to support the incident response process. Equally important, internal communication channels should be developed to keep staff informed of the incident and how they can help to expedite the recovery effort.

A key aspect of the BCMS is the management of BCM documents. Standardized procedures for documentation management should be developed to provide assurance that controlled documents are adequately stored and maintained, and readily available for use by authorized BCM staff.

Resource allocation

Implementing any corporate project will have an impact on the manner in which resources are utilized in the organization. Similar to other management systems, the BCMS requires dedicated resources to develop the corporate business continuity capability. It is essential that the senior leadership team ensures that adequate resources are provided to establish and maintain the BCMS.

A key point to note is that the most appropriate resource management structure is often one that balances commitment and cost for the organization's BCMS. This means that the organization needs to determine the number of staff (whether full- or part-time/internal or external) and other supporting resources committed for the BCMS. In most cases, this information is determined during the project planning phase, which formalizes a realistic view of the resources required to implement the management system.

Though the functionality of technologies is an important element of the BCMS, it is the level of staff competence that dictates the value BCM brings to the organization. To put it succinctly, technological infrastructures are process enablers, whilst staff are the main driver that ensures the BCMS remains effective.

Practices of BCM professionals

Being an executive-driven initiative, the BCMS should be responsive to new organizational changes. As mentioned earlier in the book, the BCMS is an iterative management process. Individual processes need to be adequately staffed to maintain its suitability to the organization. Early delegation of tasks to key individuals ensures that the BCMS is well resourced and can help to generate a positive ownership. In most cases, the specification of BCM roles, including responsibilities, are dictated by the management tasks of the BCMS. As such, job descriptions should be developed to specify the required level of skills, education and experience for managing the BCMS.

The professional practices

The Disaster Recovery Institute (DRI) International and the Business Continuity Institute (BCI) are the world's leading professional bodies for BCM. The two institutes are widely regarded as the advocates that shape the professionalism of the industry and advance the knowledge of the subject matter. Each institute has developed a set of professional practices. In essence, the purpose of these professional practices is twofold: they specify the competence of a BCM professional, and they are designed as operating frameworks in establishing an organization's BCM programme.

The DRI has developed 10 professional practices for developing BCM proficiency. The professional practices detail the roles and activities that are essential in establishing the BCM programme. Furthermore, they offer guidance to organizations on the assessment of their programmes against accepted and proven practices. In contrast, the BCI has developed the Good Practice Guidelines, which spells out six professional practices in managing BCM activities. They are classified into two themes, namely, management and technical. The six professional practices reflect the whole lifecycle of the BCM programme, which is adaptable to fit the specific context of an organization. Table 6.1 shows the professional practices of the two institutes.

TABLE 6.1 Professional practices of Disaster Recovery Institute and Business Continuity Institute

Disaster Recovery Institute 10 Professional Practices	Business Continuity Institute 6 Professional Practices
1. Programme Initiation and Management	**Management practices**
2. Risk Evaluation and Control	1. Policy and Programme Management
3. Business Impact Analysis	2. Embedding Business Continuity
4. Business Continuity Strategies	**Technical practices**
5. Emergency Response and Operations	3. Analysis
6. Plan Implementation and Documentation	4. Design
7. Awareness and Training Programmes	5. Implementation
8. Business Continuity Plan Exercise, Audit and Maintenance	6. Validation
9. Crisis Communications	
10. Coordination with External Agencies	

Skills of BCM professionals

Despite some variants between the professional practices, both sets of practices can be broadly grouped into five types of organizational skills. They encapsulate what are essential in the development and management of an effective BCMS. The skills are not presented in any particular order of importance; rather, a combination of skills is required to complete a BCM activity. The skills are as follows:

- Management
- Leadership
- Communication
- Analysis
- Coordination

Management

By nature, establishing the BCMS is a series of interrelating activities with defined deliverables. BCM professionals provide oversight of the management system by ensuring that the activities are carried out appropriately to achieve the defined objectives. In the broadest sense, managerial capability comprises organizational management, role assignment, resource and time allocation, and problem management.

Leadership

Leadership prepares the organization before and during an incident. Complemented with other skills, leadership plays a dominant role in the management of the BCMS. It pertains to the skills in raising the profile of business continuity across the organization. More important, it enables the BCM professional to assume the leading role in managing the recovery process during an incident.

Communication

Communication skills account for a major part of BCM activities. The primary role of BCM professionals is to engage staff and external stakeholders in all aspects of the BCMS. The ability to communicate effectively ensures that information is disseminated to those who require it for decision-making as well as those responsible for implementing BCM strategies during an incident.

Analysis

Analytical skills are important in managing the BCMS, in particular, for the process of business impact analysis and risk assessment. These skills establish a logical approach to solve complex problems whilst developing informed, objective mitigation options.

Coordination

Coordination is about the planning and arrangement of BCM tasks into a proper order of relationship to achieve the defined outcomes.

They are essential when liaising with external agencies on matters relating to joint recovery operations. The skills also entail the coordination of activities that strengthen the position of business continuity in the organization, such as awareness, training and exercises.

Figure 6.1 is a depiction of the relationship between the five categories of skills and the professional practices.

Performance appraisal

A key aspect of maintaining the BCMS is the assessment of staff capability, which is also known as performance appraisal. The underlying principle of this process is to identify existing gaps and determine training and development needs to underpin the individual's competence. It also provides the basis for key managerial decisions, such as assigning roles and levels of autonomy, reviewing monetary rewards and planned career progression.

It is a norm that most organizations undertake performance appraisal on an annual basis; however, the frequency is often influenced by human resource issues, such as new members of staff joining the BCM team and those who were recently promoted or assigned to new roles with BCM responsibilities.

A key point to note is that the BCM performance appraisal should not be viewed as an independent management activity but one that relates to the corporate requirements. It should maintain ongoing review and, where necessary, align staff competence to address challenges in the organization's operating environment.

Approaches to performance appraisal

Fundamentally, performance appraisal is used to assess attitudes, behaviour and capability. Broadly, there are two types of evaluation to appraise staff:

- Rating scale/checklist method
- SMART method

FIGURE 6.1 Relationship between management skills and professional practices

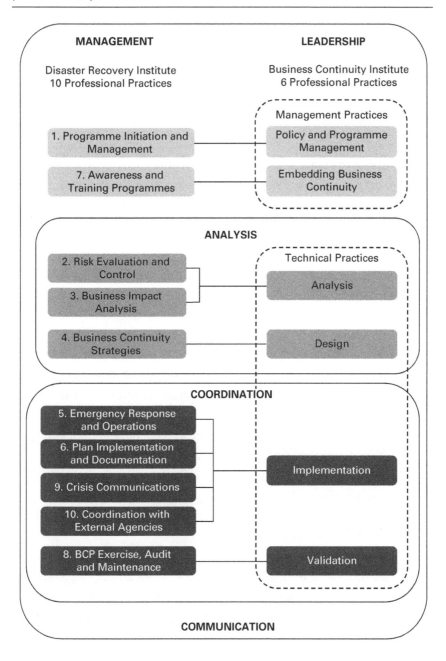

Rating scale/checklist method

The rating scale/checklist method establishes an absolute form of measurement. A rating scale such as 1 (unsatisfactory) to 5 (excellence) is used to evaluate the performance of the individual who is responsible for the BCMS. Alternatively, a checklist of criteria grouped under several headings can be used to determine if the set objectives have been fulfilled. To ensure that this method can yield meaningful results, the incorporation of an analytical coded technique in the rating scale can provide further explanation of the score. The use of a point system in checklists could also establish the causal factors of performance, which helps to identify areas of attention. In most cases, this method is used as a preliminary form of evaluation prior to an in-depth qualitative appraisal.

SMART method

The SMART method entails the use of unstructured narrative style to inform specific factors and the overall work performance. It is the most common approach adopted by managers, in which they agree upon a set of defined objectives with staff under review. These objectives are derived from the SMART concepts, that is, specific, measurable, achievable, realistic and time-bound. They are set out according to the individual's roles and responsibilities in the BCMS. The appraisal is based upon the extent to which the agreed objectives have been met. In order to ensure an unbiased assessment, it is important that evidence is used to substantiate the claim.

Though each method offers its value in understanding staff performance, a combined approach is perhaps a far better option since they enable the performance appraisal to be carried out in a more objective and conclusive manner.

In the context of business continuity, the incorporation of a series of key performance indicators (KPIs) can act as guidance to develop incentives or reward those who fulfil the defined performance criteria. These KPIs can be used to assess an individual's BCM competence. They are developed based on five key areas:

- Core skills – The ability to plan and manage BCM activities
- Technical expertise – The knowledge of BCM and its methodology

- Process development – The ability to develop and implement BCM activities in accordance to the business continuity policy
- Communication – The ability to engage with internal and external stakeholders in a range of BCM activities
- Knowledge management – The knowledge of managing business continuity materials and the document lifecycle

It is important to note that performance appraisal must be supported by follow-up actions. For instance, changes in roles and responsibilities are actually taking place as agreed upon or appropriate arrangements are being developed to address competence issues.

Continual development

Continual development of staff competence is one of the most critical drivers in sustaining the integrity of the BCMS. It comprises training and development, which help to instil confidence, motivation and commitment amongst BCM staff. Continual development reconciles the gap between actual levels of work performance and desired expectations defined in the performance appraisal. Executive support for the ongoing enhancement of knowledge and skills of those responsible for the BCMS is important.

It is becoming a growing trend that organizations with established BCM programmes invest in training and development for their BCM staff. Training is primarily concerned with the acquisition of new skills or extending individual capability in particular areas, such as business continuity in information and communications technology. This often emphasizes short- to medium-term skills that could become obsolete as new developments emerge in the BCM industry. In contrast, development is about the continual enhancement of personal and other human-centric abilities, such as the five managerial skills mentioned earlier in the chapter; development tends to focus on long-term issues of managing the BCMS.

It is important to note that training and development are not mutually exclusive; neither one is sufficient to equip the challenging role of a BCM professional. In most cases, the training element is embedded as part of staff's long-term development programme, also known as the continuous professional development (CPD). This is often an essential feature of holding a professional qualification – a prerequisite to retain membership with a professional institution. Broadly, the key areas of training and development include the following:

- BCM activities – This refers to specific skills in undertaking activities, such as business impact analysis and risk assessment, strategies formulation and selection, plans development and project/programme management.
- Organizational management – This primarily focuses on organizational skills, such as leadership theories, management practices and organizational behaviour.
- Change management – This refers to skills in identifying corporate change drivers and implementing change management techniques.
- Process optimization – This refers to skills in assessing and improving BCM activities, such as performance evaluation, audit and benchmarking study.
- Exercise and testing – This refers to the skills in validating BCM arrangements, such as planning and facilitating different levels of exercise, note taking and post-exercise debrief.

Business continuity awareness and training programme

Though the ongoing improvement of the BCM team is a significant leap for the BCMS, an adequate BCMS cannot be established fully without attention to increasing the knowledge and skills of general staff. This comes in the form of a programme that comprises two interrelating activities: awareness and training. The former aims to raise the understanding of general staff about the whole subject of business continuity whilst the latter equips those who have BCM roles with the necessary skills to undertake specific activities.

The programme emphasizes the importance of staff conformance with the business continuity policy and ensures tasks are carried out in a consistent manner. In essence, compliance is derived from a fully aware and adequately trained workforce.

As the specialist group that manages the BCMS, the BCM team is often tasked with implementing the BCMS awareness and training programme. Because of the varied nature of organizations, four key areas should be considered when establishing the programme activities:

- The size and geographic dispersion of organizational functions
- The corporate incident management structure
- The roles and responsibilities of staff during an incident
- The budget allocation for the programme

In the broadest sense, establishing activities of a business continuity awareness and training programme can be divided into four stages:

1 Design the awareness and training programme

2 Develop awareness and training materials

3 Implement the awareness and training programme

4 Evaluate the awareness and training programme

It is important to note that communication forms a crucial part of the awareness and training programme since it underpins the implementation and evaluation phases of the programme.

Figure 6.2 illustrates the lifecycle of the business continuity awareness and training programme.

FIGURE 6.2 Lifecycle of business continuity awareness and training programme

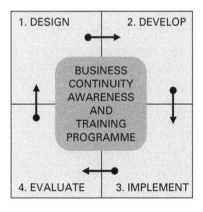

Design the awareness and training programme

It is important to consider the current state of the organization's BCMS and the culture that supports it when designing an awareness and training programme. The design stage comprises three activities:

- Conduct a training needs analysis
- Develop an awareness and training strategy plan
- Identify priorities

Conduct a training needs analysis

A training needs analysis (TNA) is often used to identify gaps in staff knowledge and skills. Basically, it helps to address five questions:

- Gaps: What is the current level of BCM knowledge and skills compared to the desired level?
- Requirements: What are needed in the current awareness and training programme?
- Arrangements: What have been done and what need to be improved?
- Adequacy: How effective are the current awareness and training activities?
- Priorities: What awareness and training needs are the most critical?

A key aspect of this activity is to identify the target audience. Broadly, there are four groups of audience:

- Executive management – Members at board level need to appreciate the function of business continuity in the organization. There should be some form of briefing to help them to understand their leadership roles in contributing to the effectiveness of the BCMS.
- Staff with specific BCM responsibilities – This group of staff usually comprises the BCM representatives of organizational functions. Though they do not hold full-time BCM responsibilities, they may undertake incident response roles, such as fire evacuation, damage assessment and business-

level BCM leadership. They therefore need to be trained with specific skills to support the central BCM team before, during and after the incident.

- General staff – The majority of the workforce needs to understand the value of business continuity in safeguarding the organization's critical processes. They need to be briefed on how they can contribute to its intended outcomes. In addition, basic knowledge about business continuity and other related issues, such as responding to specific threats and building evacuations, should form part of their awareness and training programme.

- Critical vendors – This group of stakeholders needs a high degree of business continuity awareness since they are part of the organization's delivery network. Depending on the nature of their role, they may be required to undergo specific training to heighten their business continuity capability.

Table 6.2 provides a list of suggested sources of information and their methods of collection as part of the needs assessment.

TABLE 6.2 Sources and methods of information collection

Sources of Information	Methods of Collection
Interview with key stakeholder groups	• This includes in-depth discussions with senior management, business directors and business continuity plan (BCP) owners to understand what has been done.
Past TNA reports	• Assess if the defined levels of awareness and training have been achieved.
Awareness and training materials	• Review existing awareness and training documents, training schedules and target audience list. Identify areas of deficiencies/ improvements based on the TNA.

(Continued)

TABLE 6.2 (*Continued*)

Sources of Information	Methods of Collection
High-level discussions with decision-makers	• Engage top management and key representatives of organizational functions to determine awareness and training needs.
Internal reviews/ audits	• Review any requirements or recommendations pertaining to business continuity awareness and training in the organization.
Business continuity policy	• Review the requirements in the policy and determine the level of corporate compliance.
Past incident reports	• Analyze actual incidents and near-misses, and identify specific groups of staff and their potential needs for awareness and training.
Corporate governance	• Assess the extent to which the business continuity policy has been aligned with the corporate requirements. Identify if resilience issues are addressed in the requirements.
BCM documents	• Review business-level exercise reports and check if follow-up actions have been completed. Determine if the frequency of exercise, maintenance and plans updates have been followed in accordance to the business continuity policy.
Industry reports	• Identify good practices pertaining to business continuity awareness and training requirements. This can provide insights on how the organization can adopt the changes to enhance the programme.

Based on the TNA, the findings are used to establish the relationship between the organization's current coverage and the desired awareness and training requirements (Figure 6.3). The gap highlights areas where further business continuity awareness and training activities need to be taken to achieve the desired level.

FIGURE 6.3 Gap analysis of business continuity awareness and training needs

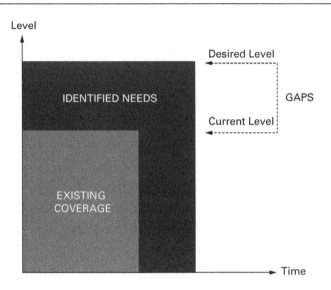

Develop an awareness and training strategy plan

Once the TNA is completed, a strategy is developed for designing and implementing the business continuity awareness and training programme. This is usually supported by a plan that comprises a series of elements:

- Scope and objectives of the programme – The defined coverage of awareness and training activities. These activities should directly contribute to the achievement of the overall purpose of the programme. A decision has to be made whether the programme covers the entire organization or focuses on key functions and individuals.

- Business continuity objectives – The awareness and training programme should align with and address the objectives and requirements of the business continuity policy.

- Target audience – The defined group of functions or individuals that are required to participate in the awareness and training programme. It is important to involve external vendors in the awareness and training activities.

- Awareness and training activities – The types of activities that impart BCM knowledge and skills. Generally, these include corporate inductions, workshops, seminars, training sessions and clinics.

- Awareness and training materials – The material content normally includes the topic, the body of knowledge to be assimilated, the structure of the activity and learning objectives and outcomes.

- Mode of delivery – This addresses how the awareness and training activity is to be delivered: face-to-face, virtual or online.

- Communication structure – The communication between the programme delivery team and the participants. This is commonly in the form of feedback via evaluation forms, focus groups or selective interviews.

- Frequency – The planned intervals at which the target audience should undergo the awareness and training sessions. In most cases, because of time and resource constraints, a 12-month cycle is used. It is worth noting that a continuous programme rather than a one-off event proves to be a more effective approach since interest in business continuity is sustained by a series of activities spread throughout the year. However, those with key BCM roles in their functions should undergo ad hoc training sessions as required.

- Planned reviews – The content of the materials should be reviewed and updated at least annually or when there are new developments in the BCM industry.

Identify priorities

A schedule of awareness and training activities can be established once the strategy and plan are completed. However, priorities are often influenced by a number of factors:

- BCM knowledge and skills – In cases where the appreciation of business continuity is relatively limited or there is a lack of BCM knowledge and skills in the organization, awareness campaigns would prove to be an effective instrument to pave the way for training activities. On the other hand, if an organization has an established BCM programme, a series of customized training sessions could reinforce staff competence and confidence.

- Management priority – In many cases, the sequence of awareness and training activities are influenced by the corporate focus of executive management. If there is a recent near-miss or incident at one of the locations, it may be regarded as a high priority to devise broad-based awareness campaigns that cover key BCM issues, such as promoting good BCM practices in key processes. Alternatively, critical functions may receive priority in the BCMS rollout strategy because of their role in generating high-value products and services.

- Resources – If there are adequate resources, including funding and staff time, a number of key awareness and training initiatives can be implemented in parallel. However, in any case where essential resources cannot be secured, priorities need to be rescheduled.

- External influences – External drivers such as corporate incidents or new statutory regulations pertaining business continuity can prompt organizations to re-examine their level of preparedness. Such influences can act as an impetus for business continuity awareness and training activities.

- Current state of development – This refers to the gaps in the awareness and training programme – what is currently being done and what is required. In order to narrow the gaps, the focus should be to address those deficiencies that can impede the effective implementation of key BCM activities.

- Dependencies – If there are tasks dependent upon a segment of training in order to proceed in the BCMS project, such as conducting a business impact analysis and risk assessment training prior to undertaking organizational and business analysis, the training schedule needs to ensure that the training activity takes place within the defined timescale.

Develop awareness and training materials

When designing awareness and training materials, two interrelating issues should be considered:

- What form of knowledge needs to be introduced in the organization's BCMS – Awareness
- What skills do the target audience need to acquire to support the implementation of the BCMS – Training

Staff across the organization should be included in business continuity awareness campaigns. The awareness materials should make them understand their commonly shared responsibility in the organization's BCMS. In contrast, training materials are designed for specific staff who hold BCM roles in their respective functions. They include key instructions pertaining to particular skills the individual needs to acquire in order to perform the required tasks.

The development stage consists of the following:

- Design awareness and training materials
- Business continuity awareness and training topics

Design awareness and training materials At the outset, a decision must be made as to the level of difficulty in the delivery materials. This should be based on two considerations: the roles of the target audience and the level of competence required for undertaking the BCM tasks. The messages in awareness materials should be written in layman terms. They should promote good BCM practices and emphasize the benefits BCM adds to organizational processes.

In contrast, training materials should be developed with a specific audience in mind. They encapsulate specific skills participants need to acquire in order to support the work of the BCM team. The materials should be instructive and enable those who attended the session to confidently assume their BCM roles.

Business continuity awareness and training topics Depending on the requirements identified in the TNA, there are a range of topics that can be incorporated into the awareness and training activities. The following proposed areas are not an exhaustive list; rather, they suggest some useful themes that the BCM team can adopt when designing the awareness and training materials.

Awareness programme

- The subject of BCM: its definition, purpose, objectives and benefits
- Introduction to BCM documents and activities
- BCM roles and responsibilities of general staff
- BCM and corporate culture
- Embedment of BCM in organizational activities

Training programme

- Business impact analysis and risk assessment
- Risk management
- BCM strategies and BCP development
- BCM exercise development and management
- Crisis and incident management
- BCM and disaster recovery
- BCM in supply chain

Implement the awareness and training programme

Prior to implementing the awareness and training programme, it is imperative to gain executive management's endorsement and funding support. The awareness and training plan also needs to be communicated to staff across the organization to gain their support. This includes explaining the objectives, benefits and desired outcomes of the programme.

The development stage consists of:

- Methods for delivering awareness activities
- Methods for delivering training activities

There are a variety of methods that can be adopted to deliver awareness and training activities. In most cases, the methods selected are dictated by the availability of resources as well as the complexity of the activity.

Methods for delivering awareness activities Some methods are simple and fairly inexpensive to implement, ranging from posters to group-wide email messages, which can disseminate a single message. On the other hand, methods such as newsletters and web-based sessions may require more resources and time to develop. One effective approach to sustain the interest of the target audience is to deploy a variety of methods. This enhances the level of understanding whilst providing a lasting impact to the audience. For instance, the use of posters supported by newsletters and email can reinforce the message.

Methods for delivering training activities   When selecting the methods for delivering training, the following factors should be considered:

- Ease of use – From the instructor's perspective, it is important that the method can be updated and tailored to support the BCM training session. While for the users, it should be easy to access and use.
- Flexibility – The method is able to deliver to a number of users based at a single office or a large group of users spread across different locations.
- Support – This is often important in the development of web-based or interactive learning packages. Support is influenced by factors such as the availability of in-house experts and the organization's technological capability. The central BCM team may consider engaging external vendors to support certain training activities, such as qualified BCM instructors to deliver onsite instructor-led training.

Combining a number of methods in one training activity can be an effective way to improve the learning experience of participants. The following table summarizes the common methods of delivery for the awareness and training programme (Table 6.3).

TABLE 6.3 Methods of delivery for awareness and training activities

Methods of Delivery (Awareness Activities)	Methods of Delivery (Training Activities)
• Posters	• Instructor-led sessions
• Organization-wide email messages	• Web-based training (online)
• Newsletters	• Interactive video training
• Web-based sessions	• Customized training packages (offline)
• Lunch-time talks	
• Free gifts inscribed with key messages	• Mentoring
• BCM day event	
• Pamphlets	

Evaluate the awareness and training programme

Continual improvement should be a central theme for the business continuity awareness and training programme. This ensures that the programme remains supportive and relevant to the requirements of the BCMS. In essence, there are two crucial components of continual improvement: evaluation and feedback.

Evaluation focuses on the review of the whole lifecycle of the awareness and training programme. The use of industry-wide good practices is a useful approach when conducting the evaluation. This helps to identify gaps in the programme and determine measures to improve the management activities, for instance, identifying improvements to existing processes of undertaking a TNA.

In contrast, feedback is designed to address the objectives of the awareness and training programme, which provides refinements to the strategy and plan. In most cases, it is used to address key aspects of the awareness or training session from the participant perspective, such as the methods of delivery, level of difficulty, duration and relevancy of sessions. Common methods of feedback include questionnaires, evaluation forms, focus groups and selective interviews.

Change management

The awareness and training programme is an integral part of the organization's BCMS. When there are changes in the requirements of the business continuity policy, it is important that the programme, together with its activities and materials, is reviewed to reflect the currency of the BCMS. New developments in business continuity will need to be disseminated throughout the organization at all levels using various awareness activities. This helps improve staff understanding of the subject as well as sustaining their ongoing commitment to the BCMS. In addition, training needs will need to be revisited to incorporate new knowledge and skills in the training activities in order to maintain the competence of those with BCM roles.

Principles of communication

Effective communication is one of the critical aspects of the BCMS. It improves the decision-making process during an incident and is concerned with building relationships with key stakeholders through information-sharing activities. It is important that during the design of the communication structure, internal and external stakeholders and their information requirements are determined. In the broadest sense, communication comprises two phases: preparatory and incident management, which encapsulate the procedures for disseminating, receiving and responding to relevant information.

During the preparatory phase, the organization works jointly with external agencies to identify information requirements, such as warnings, incident updates and recovery strategies. These requirements are then incorporated into the communication protocols that help to establish a mutual understanding about one another's roles and actions in the incident management process.

In the incident management phase, organizations implement the agreed-upon communication protocols in a consistent manner. Information received is used for making key decisions on appropriate actions. The emphasis is to minimize unnecessary delays in communication and facilitate a concerted approach to incident management.

There are four factors organizations should consider when developing protocols for information sharing:

- Content – What is the purpose of the information and what does it entail?
- Timing – When should the information be transmitted?
- Stakeholders – Who should receive the information?
- Type of communication methods – How is the information disseminated?

In most cases, the communication structure is influenced by the organization's command and control hierarchy: strategic, tactical and operational. It is important that information content, such as message templates, are tailored to meet the requirements of different stakeholders. Equally important, communication protocols should be exercised to ensure that they can be effectively invoked at short notice following an incident.

Internal communication

An appropriate internal communication structure should be established for managing information between various groups of stakeholders in the organization. This includes communication channels used to provide updates and explain to staff what is required of them to support the business continuity and recovery process. In addition, there should be documented handover and briefing procedures to ensure staff are fully informed of the situation before assuming command.

The key messages for staff and key suppliers include the following:

- How the incident affects them – their safety and welfare are of the utmost importance
- How they can support critical organizational requirements – their roles in the business continuity and recovery process
- Alternative forms of working – this includes home working, or working at alternate locations or client offices

External communication

The objective of establishing the organization's external communication protocols is to ensure that key stakeholders are aware of and prepared for the measures that they need to take during an abnormal situation. All communication activities should serve to demonstrate the organization's ability to continue its critical operations following an incident. The protocols should ensure the reliability of information received and disseminated. In addition, due to the dynamism of an incident, the protocols should remain flexible to support the organization's position when transmitting information.

The key messages for external stakeholders include the following:

- How the organization is maintaining 'business-as-usual' under the prevailing conditions
- Key corporate priorities, whilst ensuring the ongoing safety and well-being of staff affected by the incident
- Where and when further information updates can be found regarding the organization's management of the incident (if applicable)

Equally important is that information, including alerts and response actions related to potential incidents, is shared efficiently between the organization's command and control team and their equivalents at other responder organizations. This ensures that key decisions are made collectively and that joint responses can be implemented in a timely fashion.

Communication with the media

The media interest in any major incident is likely to be very high. There should be a trained individual, also known as the spokesperson, to manage the communication process to the media. All information should be channelled through a single source in order to ensure the messages are consistently delivered. Staff should ensure that procedures are adhered to when cascading information to relevant individuals within the organization or when they are approached by the media for comments.

In a multi-agency response, the organization's spokesperson will prepare the information for public release and consult with counterparts at other organizations, if necessary. They will collectively ensure that a consistent message is transmitted to the media and general public. Consideration should also be given to the tone and content of the message as well as methods used prior to dissemination.

Figure 6.4 illustrates a simplified diagram of the organization's external and internal communication structure.

BCMS documentation management

Documentation is the administration of documentary materials that support the organization's BCMS. It involves a systematic lifecycle management of business continuity materials: the creation, update and control of documented information. Its functions are to regulate changes to key documents in a controlled manner and give authorized individuals access to the latest version of the documents. Like any management system, the level of detail in documentation should reflect the nature of the BCMS. It should adequately describe the operation of the BCMS and how key documents fit together to effect the business continuity capability. For an audit, an established documentation system provides evidence of a well-managed BCMS.

A number of factors should be considered prior to the development of a documentation management system:

- The nature of the organization – The size and type of business operations will often determine how the BCMS is managed. For organizations with diverse operations or that are geographically dispersed, the number and types of BCM documents will significantly differ from organizations that operate in a single location with less complex activities.

- The complexity of the BCMS – Depending on the scope of the BCMS, the documentation hierarchy is influenced by the different types of plans and reports generated by BCM activities, as well as the interface between various plans.

- Knowledge and skills of the BCM team – Good knowledge in information security and knowledge management can greatly enhance the process of documentation management.

FIGURE 6.4 Simplistic external and internal communication structure

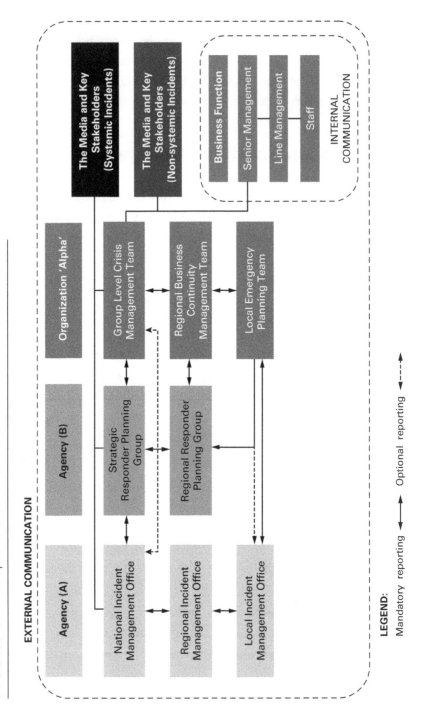

LEGEND:

Mandatory reporting ←→   Optional reporting ←---→

Principles of documentation management

It is important to note the following concepts when devising procedures for the documentation management system:

- Document control
- Version control
- Roles and responsibilities
- Storage and disposal

Document control

The purpose of document control is to ensure that documentary information is current and the confidentiality of business continuity materials is safeguarded. Key aspects of document control include the review of documents by authorized personnel, change control, distribution and storage, and the elimination of obsolete documents.

Examples of documents that require control follow:

- Business continuity policy
- BCM staff information and associated competency and training records
- Business impact analysis and risk assessment reports
- BCM strategies
- BCPs and other related plans
- Exercise and testing reports
- Management review reports
- Audit reports

Version control

The BCM documents are subject to ongoing review at planned intervals or more regularly if there are significant changes to organizational activities. There should be version control in each reviewed document. Version control provides easy identification of each subsequent version, whether electronic or paper copy. The version number changes as the document is revised, allowing released versions of a document to be readily discernible from draft or earlier versions. In practice, documents may be identified by a version number starting at one and increasing by one for each release. For instance, ver. 1.0 (original) to ver. 1.1 (minor changes) or ver. 2.0 (major changes/new version). However, this is up to the reviewer's discretion. In addition, the information in the distribution list should be updated if controlled copies are to be distributed.

Typical examples of distribution list before and after revision are illustrated in Tables 6.4 and 6.5, respectively.

TABLE 6.4 Version number prior to revision

Distribution:

Copy No.	Version	Issue date	Issue to
1	1.0	09/05/2012	BCM Director, Risk and Control Division
2	1.0	09/05/2012	BC Manager, Risk and Control Division
3	1.0	09/05/2012	Deputy BC Manager, Risk and Control Division
Electronic	1.0	07/05/2012	Shared drive

TABLE 6.5 Version number after major revision

Distribution:

Copy No.	Version	Issue date	Issue to
1	2.0	11/02/2013	BCM Director, Risk and Control Division
2	2.0	11/02/2013	BC Manager, Risk and Control Division
3	2.0	11/02/2013	Deputy BC Manager, Risk and Control Division
Electronic	2.0	09/02/2013	Shared drive

Roles and responsibilities

In most cases, it is the central BCM team that is responsible for documentation management. The team determines the level of document control to be used in the BCMS. Key documents, such as business impact analysis/risk assessment reports and BCPs, usually require a higher degree of document control since they contain sensitive information relating to the organization's key processes and strategies. It is important that individual teams that develop their respective BCM documents adhere to the relevant control procedures established by the central BCM team. In some cases, the business continuity steering committee may include additional controls to underpin the documentation management process.

The same authorized personnel who reviewed and approved the original document, unless the control procedures specifically allow otherwise, should review changes to the information in the document. Changes should be promptly distributed to the central team and other parties concerned, along with a master list enumerating the revisions of each document.

Storage and disposal

The essence of an effective documentation management process is to ensure the constant availability of key BCM documents. Like other organizational activities, the BCMS is a document-driven process and requires defined procedures to manage the whole lifecycle of business continuity materials. Regardless of electronic and paper versions of the document, it is important to consider the following factors:

- Storage and retrieval
- Location
- Security
- Disposal

Storage and retrieval

Good storage equals good access. A key element in this process is a robust storage and backup regime. Most BCM documents are created electronically and stored in the organization's central server or the hard drive. They should be arranged and labelled in such a manner that they can be retrieved efficiently. It is important that all sensitive documents follow the corporate policy on the management and dissemination of confidential information or the documentation management guidance described at the beginning of this section. For authorized staff, it is prudent to have their backup version in portable drives, such as USB flash drives and storage media, and a paper version of the plan with them. This provides assurance in situations where their primary place of work becomes inaccessible or they are required to lead the recovery process during out-of-office hours.

Location

Documents that are active should be stored in the most appropriate location for their purpose, which would normally be the place of work for the BCM staff. It is important to have backup versions stored away from the primary workplace, preferably at a secondary location or an alternate office. As a matter of good business management, most organizations should have adequate disaster recovery measures to support such arrangement (details on the subject are beyond the scope of this book). However, a point to note regarding the geographical dispersion of storage locations: whilst greater distance usually reduces the likelihood of two sites being affected by the same incident, there are certain threats such as systemic power outages and viruses that find no borders. Nonetheless, for conventional physical incidents, a few hundred metres is unlikely to provide secured protection for key documents.

Security

The degree of security required for storage will depend on the sensitivity of business continuity materials. In most cases, BCM reports, plans and third-party contracts are considered protected materials, which should be stored as securely as possible in order to avoid potential misuse or loss. In particular, paper versions should be locked up when not in use. Electronic documents should be subject to the same restriction of access as protected paper documents. The media upon which they are held, such as hard drive, must be capable of incorporating passwords to restrict access.

Disposal

The process of disposal is influenced by the method in which the documents are stored. Organizations should set out procedures for eliminating obsolete materials from each location and identifying any superseded documents retained for record. Electronic documents should be either stored in the permanent archive or deleted according to the corporate record retention and disposal policy. All deleted records should also have primary and backup copies removed at the same time. This measure ensures that the BCMS is based on the latest version of the documents, which also minimizes the unintended use of obsolete information. Likewise, paper documents should be checked and disposed of according to the organization's policy for classified waste disposal, usually by paper shredders, specialist waste contractors or special waste carriers for papers and multimedia objects.

Summary

Regardless of the size, nature and complexity of an organization, an effective BCMS is influenced by a number of factors, namely, resource support, staff competence, awareness and training programme, and incident communication structure. In addition, a well-managed BCMS is supported by an appropriate documentation regime that regulates revisions of business continuity materials in a consistent manner whilst ensuring that authorized personnel have access to the most up-to-date plans during an incident.

CHECKLIST

This checklist is intended to support the business continuity management system (BCMS) development process	Yes	No	Action required
Does the organization's BCMS incorporate the allocation of dedicated resources and finance as a part of the annual budget development and management process?	❏	❏	❏
Are qualified BCM professionals involved in the implementation and management of the organization's BCMS?	❏	❏	❏
Are performance appraisals in place to assess the adequacy of BCM staff competence?	❏	❏	❏
Does the organization have a business continuity awareness and training programme?	❏	❏	❏
Have the business continuity policy, requirements and the BCMS been communicated throughout the organization?	❏	❏	❏
Does the organization have a defined external and internal communication structure during an incident?	❏	❏	❏
Does the organization have defined process and procedures to communicate with staff and key suppliers?	❏	❏	❏
Does the organization have defined process and procedures to communicate with external agencies?	❏	❏	❏
Does the organization have a clearly defined media and public relations strategy and plan?	❏	❏	❏
Has the organization identified the key stakeholders and interest groups?	❏	❏	❏
Does the organization have a clearly defined and approved BCMS documentation management system?	❏	❏	❏

References

Business Continuity Institute (2013) *Good Practice Guidelines: A guide to global good practice in business continuity*, Business Continuity Institute, Caversham

Disaster Recovery Institute International (DRII) (2012) *Professional Practices for Business Continuity Practitioners*, DRII, New York

Further reading

ISO 22301:2012 – Societal security – Business continuity management systems – Requirements

ISO 22313:2012 – Societal security – Business continuity management systems – Guidance

Operation

07

OVERVIEW

- This chapter first outlines the essential attributes of understanding the organization.
- It then explains the key characteristics and concepts of a business impact analysis and how to undertake the activity.
- Next, it discusses the key characteristics and concepts of a risk assessment and its key approaches.
- The chapter goes on to introduce business continuity strategy selection and development, and explains the stages, approaches and key resources of establishing appropriate BCM strategies.
- Furthermore, it explains how to establish the business continuity capability, which includes developing the incident management structure and plans.
- Finally, the chapter highlights the different levels of validating the organization's business continuity capability and explains the key roles in the exercise planning team and exercise programme.

Background

A fit-for-purpose business continuity capability is based on an in-depth review of the organization and its activities. It entails assessment of the impacts to the organization of a loss of its critical operations and determining the resources required to attain their recovery time-scales. This is underpinned by a risk assessment that identifies priorities and mitigation strategies to safeguard the key operations.

In addition, there should be an appropriate form of corporate configuration for managing incidents, also known as the incident management structure (IMS), to execute command and control in the incident management process. This is to ensure that a coordinated approach is established for communication, decision-making and the implementation of responses during an incident. In its basic form, the IMS comprises strategic, tactical and operational teams, with each assigned to address different types of incidents. However, the exact composition of the corporate IMS is largely dependent on the type, size and complexity of the organization.

In order to provide greater assurance following an incident that critical operations will be recovered as required, there should be planned series of exercises to validate plans and team/individual skills. Broadly, there are two forms of exercise: discussion-based and operation-based, which can develop into five types of exercise, namely, orientation, desktop, drill, functional exercise and full-scale exercise. Each exercise is designed for different levels of BCM maturity and focuses on particular aspects of BCM. Nonetheless, as the exercise activity gains complexity, there should be risk controls to prevent probable threats from developing an exercise into a real incident. In essence, exercises provide the opportunity to identify areas of improvement, which help to drive the continual enhancement of the organization's business continuity capability.

Understanding the organization

Understanding the organization and its business forms the basis of developing a business-driven BCMS. It comprises the process of identifying the critical functions based on their impacts on the organization's ability to achieve its objectives and obligations. This is supported by a risk assessment, which ensures that the likelihood (frequency and probability) of critical functions being affected by probable threats is minimized. The findings are then used to determine the recovery priorities and formulate resilience measures to safeguard continuity.

In essence, understanding the organization comprises three inter-related activities:

- Business impact analysis (BIA) – This consists of analytical methodologies that assess the functions whose failure would most immediately threaten product and service delivery and have significant impact on the organization.

- Business continuity resource requirements analysis (BCRRA) – This activity forms an integral part of the BIA, which determines the level of resources that each critical function requires at both resumption and return to business-as-usual following a disruption.

- Risk assessment (RA) – This activity identifies potential threats to critical functions and develops risk-mitigation measures to minimize their occurrence and impact.

It is important to note that the activities of understanding the organization is performed before setting the corporate risk appetite, since it is the BIA and the subsequent RA that inform the probable impact and threats to the organization's ability to fulfil its requirements. This information also helps to prioritize where resources should be invested in the development of BCM and risk-mitigation strategies.

Characteristics of business impact analysis

The BIA assesses the qualitative and quantitative impact incurred by the organization following an incident. Fundamentally, it provides information about individual critical functions in terms of the following:

- The tangible and intangible impact over time to the organization, including reputational damage, loss of revenue and regulation breach

- The timescales in which the critical functions must be recovered

- The resource requirements to sustain a set level of functionality and operation

In essence, five key questions should be considered when defining critical functions:

- What are the corporate objectives and obligations?

- What products and services are required to achieve the corporate objectives and obligations?

- When do the corporate objectives and obligations need to be achieved?

- What is the impact if they are not achieved?
- Who are responsible for delivering the corporate objectives and obligations (both internally and externally)?

To ensure that the relationship between various parts of the organization is assessed, the BIA should be carried out in an end-to-end business service and product context. Rather than operating as independent lines of processes, many of the activities coexist internally and externally. One effective approach is to work back from the final output (product or service) in which all resources and activities that contribute to different stages of the delivery can be identified.

It is also important that internal and external factors that can affect the delivery of the organization's key products and services are considered as part of the BIA. In general, internal factors include operations and resources, and dependency relationships, whilst external factors comprise market drivers, stakeholders and supply chains.

An integral part of the BIA is a process known as business continuity resource requirements analysis (BCRRA). This process determines the resource recovery profile necessary to achieve the prioritized recovery of critical functions according to their respective recovery timescales.

Basic concepts – business impact analysis

When undertaking the BIA, it is important to develop a common understanding of the following terms in order to ensure that they are applied consistently (Table 7.1).

Develop business impact analysis project

The crucial first step in a BIA is to gain executive sponsorship for the project. In some cases, the decision about which products or services fall within the scope of the BCMS may have been made beforehand by the senior leadership team. This could be due to the revenue generated by the products or the mandatory services required by the authority. Alternatively, a holistic BIA could be conducted across the organization to seek a thorough understanding of its operations.

TABLE 7.1 Concepts of business impact analysis

Terms	Description	Units
Critical product or service	The output of the organization that fulfils its most important objectives and obligations.	
Critical function	An organized entity and its processes that deliver the critical product or service in order for the organization to fulfil its objectives and obligations. In most cases, the element of 'impact over time' is used to qualify the term.	
Time	• Maximum tolerable period of disruption (MTPD): The maximum duration in which the organization can operate without the critical function, after which the impact would become unacceptable. • Recovery time objective (RTO): The defined timescale in which the critical function must be recovered. It is important to note that the MTPD should be developed prior to the RTO. Also, the RTO should be shorter than the MTPD. • Recovery point objective (RPO): The defined point in time in which key activities should be restored after an incident in order to initiate the continuity of operation. This is generally considered as a particular time before the occurrence of an incident, such as the time when the most reliable information was available before an outage.	• Minute(s) • Hour(s) • Day(s) • Week(s) • Month(s)

(Continued)

TABLE 7.1 (*Continued*)

Terms	Description	Units
Impact	The losses to the organization. This usually comes in three forms: operational, financial and non-financial impacts (see Table 7.6).	Monetary terms
Resources	• Business continuity resource requirements analysis (BCRRA): The minimum level of resources required to meet the level of business continuity of a critical activity. • Level of business continuity (LBC): The defined minimum level of continued output of product or service in order to fulfil the organization's objectives and obligations.	%

Regardless, prior to undertaking the BIA, it is important that the objectives of the project are agreed upon and approved by executive management.

Next, a detailed schedule of activities, including timescales and deliverables, should be developed and approved by the business continuity champion. The project is then communicated to all potential participants in the BIA. A prerequisite is that these participants have an in-depth knowledge about the corporate functions and are capable of articulating their business continuity requirements.

It is worth noting that there are a number of factors that could influence the quality of the BIA:

- Executive endorsement – Due to the nature of the BIA, which requires inputs from across the organization, it is unlikely that managers and staff are willing to cooperate with or dedicate time to this activity unless it is driven from the board. As such, a high-level statement of endorsement should be developed to ensure that the entire organization is responsive and committed to the project.

- Criteria – It is important that unambiguous measurements (for quantifiable and non-quantifiable impacts) are defined to assess the impact of a potential disruption to each function over time. The criteria will be used to identify and prioritize critical functions based on their impact on the organization.

- Information collection methods – Choice of method is dependent upon the scale and complexity of the organization and its operations. This is also influenced by the skills and experience of those who conduct the BIA.

- The participants – Staff with in-depth experience and knowledge can greatly enhance the quality of information collected by providing wide-ranging aspects of the functional processes.

- Skills and experiences – This refers to the competence of members in the BCM team tasked to undertake the BIA. Adequate training should be provided prior to the project's commencement.

- Project management – A clear sequence of activities with realistic timescales and deliverables should be developed. They should also be regularly reviewed and managed by the BCM team.

Methods of information collection

In practice, the information collection methods will vary from one organization to another. Furthermore, the choice will be influenced by corporate factors, such as nature, geographical dispersion and complexity of the organization. Once selected, it is important that the method is consistently applied. In addition, consideration should be given to the following five factors of information collection:

- What information will be collected: At the minimum, the information should cover impact over time to the organization in order to identify the critical functions and the recovery priorities. The information should be capable of guiding the choice of BCM strategies.

- Who the target respondents are: This refers to staff responsible for managing the organizational functions.

- How the information is analyzed: This is particularly crucial when determining non-quantifiable impacts, such as loss of public confidence and stakeholder value. When customized software packages are used, consideration should be given to the accuracy and reliability of the analytical outputs. This factor also shapes the level of detail – depth and coverage – of the information to be collected.

- Why a particular method is selected: The preferred method should adequately address the objectives of the BIA project. Strengths and weaknesses of each method should be compared based on the criteria of reliability, objectivity and ease of analysis.

- Where additional information can be found: This information is used to corroborate the findings provided by the respondents.

The most common methods used in the BIA include the following:

1 Questionnaires

2 Personal interviews

3 Workshops

4 Documentary reviews

Questionnaires

Questionnaires are often the best way of gathering primary information to develop a general view of the corporate function. This technique consists of written questions to which respondents can respond.

There are a number of factors to consider when designing questionnaires for the BIA:

- Concise information
- Layout
- Types of question
- Level of detail

Concise information   Well-written instructions can help to improve the response rate of questionnaires. At the minimum, questionnaires should include:

- The outlined purpose of the BIA
- A statement from the board emphasizing the importance of organization-wide participation in the BIA project
- How answers will be treated
- Clear instructions as to how each question should be answered, such as how many answers can be selected
- When and how the questionnaires should be returned

Layout The appearance of the questionnaire will influence the respondent's attitude towards participation and how the individual perceives the questions. It is always useful to provide sufficient space between questions so that the questionnaire does not appear overwhelming. In addition, the use of clear headings and numbering can structure the questions.

Types of questions There are generally two types of questions: factual and opinion questions. It is important that factual questions (objectivity) form the basis of the questionnaire since there is a general tendency for opinion questions (subjectivity) to provide answers based on personal attitudes, which could skew the findings of the BIA.

Level of detail Questionnaires tend to provide a broad perspective of the organizational functions. In most cases, the depth of the questions is dependent on what information the inquirer wants to find out.

In order to maximize the usability and accuracy of questionnaires, here are some useful pointers:

- Provide the questionnaire with a concise and meaningful title.
- Keep the questionnaire as short and succinct as possible.
- Use headings and colours to classify the relevant questions.
- Provide a self-explanatory guide to respondents, such as instructions and glossary of terms.
- Make the process convenient by stating the possible duration for completing the questions at the beginning of the questionnaire.

Personal interviews

Personal interviews employ verbal questioning as its principal technique of data collection. The approach is a conversation between the inquirer and the respondent that primarily focuses on key aspects of the organizational function.

There are generally three types of personal interview, which differ in terms of the structure, purpose and depth of information to be elicited:

- Fully structured interview
- Semi-structured interview
- Unstructured interview

Fully structured interview In this form of interview, the questions are devised in a standard sequential manner. The questions are identical for every respondent. The interview is based on a highly structured interview guide. This rigid structure does not provide freedom in making adjustments to any of its elements, such as content wording or order of questions.

Semi-structured interview In a semi-structured interview, a list of questions is drafted in advance, but there is ample freedom to modify the sequence of questions based on the respondent's knowledge about the organizational function. The inquirer can adapt the wording of the question wherever there are doubts or possibly leave out certain questions. In this approach, the respondent is granted considerable liberty in expressing an opinion and also allowing the inquirer to obtain details of personal experiences, reactions and the like.

Unstructured interview There is no strict control or procedures when conducting an unstructured personal interview. In this form of interview, there are no restrictions in the sequence and wording of the questions or the interview schedule. In many cases, it is guided by some form of checklist rather than rules. The inquirer can act freely based on the responses given by the respondent. It is a dynamic and flexible approach that allows free expression of opinions. The respondent is encouraged to describe whatever seems relevant whilst revealing personal opinions based on the questions.

General principles when designing questions

Prior to developing questionnaires and personal interviews, it is important to have a clear focus on what the questions intend to achieve. The BIA objectives can be a useful guide to consider what information is required from the respondents in order to achieve those goals. A list of suggested principles is provided to assist in designing questions (Table 7.2).

A list of themes for framing questions in questionnaires and personal interviews is provided in Table 7.3.

Workshops

Workshops bring a group of people together into a discussion. This is an effective approach but requires direction and control. Direction refers to guiding the respondents through the BIA whilst facilitating the discussion with the objective of reaching a consensus about the issues discussed. In contrast, control is about keeping the workshop aligned to the agenda of the BIA whilst ensuring that the timing and objectives set for the workshop are achieved. It is also important that the workshop is steered towards a conclusion.

A number of key actions should be taken when conducting a BIA workshop:

- Establish a set of objectives for the workshop. This provides guidance on how various activities are conducted and managed.

- Prepare a checklist of information required. Identify a list of information and group items in a checklist. This ensures that all pertinent areas of information are collated in the BIA workshop (Table 7.4).

- Develop an agenda and a briefing note. These documents should be distributed before the workshop. They help to prepare participants and enable them to understand what information is required of them during the workshop.

TABLE 7.2 Suggested principles in designing questions

Principles	Methods
1. Avoid leading questions	• The questions should not prompt the respondent to a specific answer, such as 'Wouldn't you say that…', 'Isn't it fair to say…'.
2. Be specific	• Ask for one piece of information at a time. Each question should be based on a single theme. 'Double-barrelled' questions could skew the focus of the respondent. Avoid questions like 'What is the risk and impact in your function'.
3. Avoid jargon and colloquialisms	• Technical expressions used in the questions should be phrased in layman's terms.
4. Ensure answers/ options are mutually exclusive	• There should be no overlaps between answers; this is particularly important for questionnaires that provide a selection of answers. For instance, 'What is the recovery time objective for this particular process: 0–3 hours, 4–10 hours, 11–15 hours, over 15 hours', not '0–3 hours, 3–10 hours, 10–15 hours …'.

5. Question order	• Once a list of questions is developed, questions should be arranged in a logical sequence:
	  i start with easy questions and background questions
	  ii progress from general to particular questions
	  iii progress from factual to abstract questions
	  iv progress from close-ended to open-ended questions

6. Trial test the questions	• Before the questions are used in the actual information collection process, it is useful to conduct trial tests to assess the quality of the questions, whether they can be easily understood in terms of wording and instructions, and how well the questions flow in sequence.

TABLE 7.3 Key areas to be covered by business impact analysis

Functions	Impacts	Recovery Timescales	Threats	Resource Requirements	Dependencies
• Processes • Deliverables (products and services) • Delivery time due	• Operational • Financial • Non-financial	• Maximum tolerable periods of disruption (MTPD) • Recovery time objectives (RTOs) • Recovery point objectives (RPOs)	• Types • Likelihood • Mitigation measures	• Level of business continuity (LBC) • People/Skills • Premises • Information • Technologies • Supplies	• Internal • External • Suppliers and stakeholders

TABLE 7.4 Information checklist for business impact analysis workshop

Item No.	Description Background Information	✓
1	List of functions	☐
2	Process chart (in the form of process mapping)	☐
3	Key contact persons	☐
	Functional analysis	
	Potential impacts	
4	List of processes	☐
5	Deliverables (products and services)	☐
6	Delivery time due	☐
7	Impact over time	☐
8	Maximum tolerable periods of disruption (MTPD)	☐
9	Recovery time objectives (RTOs)	☐
10	Recovery point objectives (RPOs)	☐
11	Priorities	☐
12	Level of business continuity (LBC)	☐
13	Resource requirements by timescales	☐
14	Dependencies	☐
15	Stakeholders	☐
	Potential threats	
16	Likelihood	☐
17	Single points of failure	☐
18	Vulnerabilities	☐
19	Mitigation measures	☐

- Collect basic information. Prior to the workshop, an initial study in the form of questionnaires can be used to elicit general information about the participants' functions. The information is useful for developing the main topics of discussion.

- Consider criteria for participants. Since a number of key decisions will have to be reached during the workshop, the participants should be staff with substantial authority in their functions and possess intimate knowledge about the processes.

- Take notes. Throughout the workshop there should be a note-taker to record key issues and decisions made.

- Follow up on outstanding issues. All outstanding issues emerging from the workshop should be documented, tasked and followed-up on with timescales.

Documentary reviews

Documentary reviews are often used as a secondary method to support other forms of information collection methods, predominantly personal interviews and workshops. They are useful in developing a basic understanding about the corporate function under study prior to undertaking the BIA or addressing gaps in the pre-analytical stage, that is, substantiating information provided by the respondents.

The methods of information collection will, to a large extent, dictate how the BIA is conducted, which can also affect the quality of the information collected. As such, it is important to develop an understanding of their strengths and weaknesses (Table 7.5).

In order to ensure that the selected methods are capable of producing reliable findings as well as meeting the requirements of the BIA, a combined approach is often recommended since it can triangulate the findings, that is, back up the findings of one method with the findings of another. For example, at the start of the project, questionnaires can be used to gather general information about corporate functions. This is then followed up by in-depth investigations, such as interviews or a workshop session.

TABLE 7.5 Strengths and weaknesses of information collection methods for BIA

	Methods of Information Collection			
	Questionnaire	**Personal Interview**	**Workshop**	**Documentary Review**
Strengths	• Inexpensive • Produces quick results • Convenient for respondents • Consistent and uniform measure • No undue influence of the inquirer • Purpose of the BIA is conveyed to the respondents • General business issues can be accommodated within the questionnaires • Complement other information collection methods	• Good communication throughout the project • Control over the project • Flexible in the questioning process • Opportunity for clarification • Minimize the ambiguity of questions • Purpose of the BIA is conveyed to the respondents • In-depth questions can be used • Effective for time-constrained studies • Produces insightful information • Complements other information collection methods	• Good communication throughout the project • A collection of key staff at the workshop • Purpose of the BIA is conveyed to the respondents • One-off event • Generates immediate consensus • Produces insightful information	• Quick and easy accessibility • Widely available due to technological and information systems • Corroborates information provided by the respondents • Evidence-based approach • Minimizes subjectivity • Cost effective • Information based on facts and figures • Complements other information collection methods

TABLE 7.5 (*Continued*)

	Methods of Information Collection			
	Questionnaire	**Personal Interview**	**Workshop**	**Documentary Review**
Weaknesses	• Questions need to be simple • Information collected is general • Lack of oversight in the information collection process • Misinterpretation of questions possible • Inflexible • No freedom of expression • Inappropriate for inexperienced respondents	• Lack of standardization • Subjectivity of the inquirer • Reservation of the respondents – due to the face-to-face conversation • Time-consuming in analyzing information	• Difficult to arrange • Discussions requires direction and control • Different opinions and conflicting interests • Lengthy process • Considerable preparation for the workshop	• Confidentiality issues • Currency and integrity of information

Information analysis

The methodology used in analyzing the findings consists of five stages:

1 Assessment of operational and financial impacts

2 Identification of recovery timescales

3 Allocation of ratings

4 Prioritization

5 Business continuity resource requirements analysis

Assessment of operational and financial impacts

This stage primarily focuses on assessing impacts over time of the failure of individual corporate functions. These are classified into operational and financial impacts. The steps of assessment are as follows:

For operational impacts:

- Quantify the impacts to the organization resulting from the function being unavailable.
- Consider the unavailability of the corporate function during the most significant peak periods, such as contractual due date for delivery and financial year end closing.
- Take into account the possibility of impacts arising from non-performance of contractual agreements and regulatory breaches due to the loss of operation.

For financial and non-financial impacts:

- Perform financial analysis in relation to the operational impacts.
- Express financial impacts that result from delivery failure in monetary terms.
- Make the time periods identical with those for assessing operational impacts (see Table 7.7) for consistent analysis.
- Express financial losses in cumulative terms for each category of financial impacts.
- Consider intangible impacts that arise from loss of productivity and reputational damage due to operational impacts.

A typical list of impacts is summarized in Table 7.6.

TABLE 7.6 Types of impacts

Operational Impacts	Financial Impacts	Non-financial Impacts
• Loss of staff (key knowledge and skills) • Loss of properties • Loss of productivity • Overtime • Replacement of plants and equipment • Knock-on effects to the backup site (operational capacity and resources) • Procurement of external resources	• Loss of revenue • Prosecution of violations and financial penalties • Costly disputes that cannot be resolved satisfactorily and could result in reputational damage • Inability to secure future opportunities due to damaged reputation	• Severe damage to the corporate reputation in the marketplace • Loss of customer confidence • Loss of business competitiveness • Loss of staff morale

Identification of recovery timescales

Three forms of recovery timescales, namely, MTPD, RTO and RPO, should be identified for each corporate function. It is important that identification is consistently performed in order to establish an organization-wide view of the recovery timescales.

Five principles should be considered when identifying the recovery timescales:

- The maximum duration after the start of an incident within which the function needs to be resumed

- The time at which the function needs to be performed (at least the minimum level) in order to meet organizational requirements

- The point in time at which the function can commence the continuity of operation

- The length of time within which the function needs to be resumed to normality

- A list of interdependent functions, with their recovery timescales, that need to be maintained continuously or recovered concurrently

Allocation of ratings

The allocation of ratings stage is about the development of a scale for quantifying the impact over time for each function. The rating scale can be expressed in numerical and descriptive formats to reflect the level of impact: 1–4 with definitions: 1 (minor impact), 2 (moderate impact), 3 (significant impact) and 4 (severe impact) (Table 7.7). Alternatively, the rating might be high, medium and low.

TABLE 7.7 Impact rating table

Function: _____ Process: _____

Impacts Operational	Description	Time	Rating
Impact 1	% output loss	< 1 hour	4
Impact 2	% output loss	1–3 hours	3
Impact 3	% output loss	>3 hours–24 hours	2
Impact 4	% output loss	>24 hours–72 hours	1
Financial	**Description**	**Time**	**Rating**
Impact 1	£ amount loss	<1 hour	4
Impact 2	£ amount loss	1–3 hours	3
Impact 3	£ amount loss	>3 hours–24 hours	2
Impact 4	£ amount loss	>24 hours–72 hours	1

Note:
4: Severe
3: Significant
2: Moderate
1: Minor

Prioritization

The findings are categorized according to criticality based on a ranking table encapsulating recovery timescales and impact ratings of individual functions. This is then developed into a schedule of priorities. Table 7.8 shows a criticality ranking table prioritizing the key functions of a health and nutrition organization.

Business continuity resource requirements analysis

This stage is about the development of the business continuity resource recovery profile. It entails the determination of the minimum level of resources to achieve the defined LBC for each critical function. Table 7.9 illustrates the staged recovery of a function in terms of timescales, LBC and resource requirements. It is important that key internal and external resources are taken into consideration when establishing the resource recovery requirements of critical functions.

TABLE 7.8 Criticality ranking table

Ranking	Descriptor	Function/Process	RTO	RPO	Impact Rating
1	Critical	Online Sales and Service Support	< 30 minutes	15 minutes	4
2	Urgent	Procurements	2 hours	1 hour	3
3	Urgent	Manufacturing and Productions	3 hours	1½ hours	3
3	Urgent	Quality and Control	3 hours	1½ hours	3
4	Important	Distributions	4 hours	2 hours	2
5	Tolerable	Design	48 hours	24 hours	1

TABLE 7.9 Staged recovery table

Resource Type	Normal Requirement	Requirement by Timescale and LBC*				Remarks
		<1 Hour 75%	3 Hours 90%	24 Hours 100%	72 Hours 100%	
Staff	70	65%	75%	100%	100%	Existing workforce/backup location
Desks	70	60%	70%	90%	100%	Backup location/third-party supplier
Computers	70	60%	70%	90%	100%	Backup location/third-party supplier
Landlines	70	30%	60%	90%	100%	Telecommunication contractor
Building	1					Relocate to backup location

*Note: LBC: Level of business continuity expressed in percentage (%)

Business impact analysis report

Once the information analysis is completed, a report is prepared for the senior leadership team summarizing the results and recommendations. The purpose is to seek management support for the conclusions of the BIA and approval for the next stage of the process. In essence, a typical BIA report should include those items discussed in Table 7.1 and the following:

- A prioritized timeline of activities for the recovery of the organization's critical functions
- A prioritized recovery profile for the development of BCM strategies
- A business continuity resource requirements analysis (BCRRA) containing the necessary resources to achieve the prioritized recovery profile of critical functions
- A list of internal and external dependencies of critical functions

In general, depending on the complexity of the project, the preparation of the BIA report comprises one or more of the following activities:

- Workshop – A follow-up workshop is usually conducted to disseminate the findings to the respondents who took part in questionnaires and personal interviews.
- Report dissemination – The draft BIA report is disseminated to the respondents who participated in the information collection process. It will include the findings and a schedule of recovery priorities for their validation.
- Further refinements – The draft report is amended according to the feedback provided by the respondents.
- Presentation and approval – The report is presented to the business continuity champion and executive management to seek their organization-wide perspective and approval of the BIA findings and recommendations.

Review of business impact analysis

The BIA is not a one-time project. It should be reviewed at planned intervals, at least every 12 months. In most cases, the review is more frequent during the development stage of the BCMS since its processes are not fully integrated into organizational activities. Once the BCMS is embedded, the maintenance of the BIA becomes a standard course of procedure. The frequency of the review is also influenced by the nature of the organization and the environment in which it operates. However, there are some triggers that prompt early review:

- Change in corporate strategies
- Organizational changes and growth
- New products or services
- Reconfiguration of corporate processes, workplace or office infrastructures
- Emerging environmental drivers, such as new legislation and resilience practices

In order to ensure that the BCMS remains a board-level issue, the BIA review cycle should be communicated to executive management when and as appropriate.

Characteristics of risk assessment

The purpose of the RA is to identify and evaluate threats to the critical functions that are determined by the BIA. This is not the conventional RA that addresses the organization-wide issues of risk. It contributes to the BCMS by ensuring that risks to critical functions have been adequately analyzed. Appropriate measures are also devised to prevent factors that could cause disruptions.

When undertaking the RA, a number of questions need to be addressed:

- What can go wrong?
- What is the likelihood of that occurring?

- What are the business impacts if the risk occurs?
- Where are the risk concentrations?
- How can the risk be managed or controlled?

Basic concepts – risk assessment

An understanding of the key concepts of the RA can ensure that terms are consistently applied, which can underpin the entire RA process (Table 7.10).

TABLE 7.10 Concepts of risk assessment

Terms	Description
Risk	A potential event and its impacts. In this context, the focus is on preventing or minimizing the occurrence of negative risks.
Threat	An active process that poses a risk that can cause damages or losses to the organization and its assets – critical functions, processes and resources.
Single point of failure	A high concentration of risks present in a particular critical function. A failure can result in a series of triggering effects.
Vulnerability	A weakness or a single point of failure that can be exploited, enabling the threat to happen.
Likelihood	The probability of a threat or risk to occur.
Impact	An outcome or an effect that can impede the organization's performance or the achievement of its objectives.
Risk appetite	The amount of risk the organization is willing to accept or tolerate. This is based on informed knowledge supported by a body of evidence.
Control	A measure to reduce or eliminate the risk (likelihood and impact) from occurring.

Approaches to risk assessment

In the broadest sense, there are two approaches to undertaking the RA: the qualitative approach and the quantitative approach. The approaches differ in nature and can influence the process that will be used in analyzing risks.

Qualitative approach

The qualitative approach has a straightforward process based on informed judgement supported by appropriate guidance. It systematically assesses risks that can cause damage to organizational assets, whilst validating whether existing mitigation measures are adequate or if new strategies are required to prevent their occurrence. This approach assigns risks to a ranking system of high, medium and low or a numerical format of 1–10, according to the judgement and experience of the person undertaking the analysis. It is important to develop a set of procedures or guidance to ensure that rankings are consistently applied when undertaking the RA process.

In the context of BCM, this approach tends to be more widely adopted since the basic information on probability and impact is sufficient to form the basis for developing risk controls and mitigation strategies.

A typical qualitative RA usually includes the following elements:

- A brief description of the risk
- An overview of the risk assessment process
- The process mapping, indicating where the risk may occur
- The factors that influence it to occur
- The relationship with other risks
- The likelihood of it occurring
- The impacts that can affect the organization

Quantitative approach

This is a mathematical approach to risk analysis. To achieve an in-depth level of detail, sophisticated mathematical models are often adopted. This approach obtains numerical estimates of the identified risks from a quantitative consideration of event probabilities and consequences.

The outputs are then compared to the numerical risk criteria at the evaluation stage to determine an acceptable level of risk. In most cases, the types and choice of risk controls are influenced by the outputs generated by the mathematical models. Though this approach is effective in analyzing risk information in dynamic settings, it requires considerable availability of resources – time, money, and staff and their skills.

The following table (Table 7.11) summarizes the key attributes of the two approaches.

TABLE 7.11   Comparison between qualitative and quantitative approaches

Qualitative Approach	Quantitative Approach
Characteristics	
• Process level	• Corporate level
• Subjective evaluation of probability and impact	• Probabilistic estimates of time and cost
• Time-saving	• Time-consuming
• Quick and easy to perform	• Specific understanding of risks
• General perception of risks	
• No special software applications or tools required	• In most cases, specialized tools or models are required
Advantages	
• Easy to understand the prioritized risks	• More accurate impression of risks
• Relatively easy and cheap	• Assessment of risks and results is objective
• Methods of assessment are simple to understand and implement	• Costs-benefits analysis can be adopted for selecting the appropriate mitigation measures
• Adaptable to fit into the organization's context	
• Simple ranking of risks based on priority – frequency and impact	• Management performance can be closely monitored
• Monetary values are not determined, which simplifies the analytical process	• Data accuracy improves with experience
• Quantitative calculation of frequency and impact is not required	

(Continued)

TABLE 7.11 (*Continued*)

Qualitative Approach	Quantitative Approach
Disadvantages	
• Oversimplified view of risks • Results are general and do not provide further information about risks • Assessment of risks and results is subjective • Major risks are inadequately differentiated • Costs-benefits analysis is difficult during the selection of mitigation strategies • Quality and reliability of results depend on the knowledge and skills of the risk management team	• Lengthy and complex • Methods of assessment are complex and expensive, and require greater experience and advanced tools • Quantitative measures depend on the scope and accuracy of the defined measurement scale • In some cases, results are not precise • Methods must be supported in qualitative description • No uniformity of approach • Values of risk impacts are based on subjective opinions of people involved • Requires specialized knowledge and skills to undertake the assessment process

Risk assessment process

There are many methodologies for undertaking the RA in the BCMS. Most, however, share a series of generic stages:

- Identification
- Evaluation
- Mitigation
- Monitoring and review

Identification

Most organizations should have corporate risk registers with some form of mitigation strategy associated with the risks. Depending on the environment in which the organization operates, there are many ways of categorizing risks. In the broadest sense, they can be categorized into natural and man-made, which can be further classified into areas such as internal/external, systemic/non-systemic, controllable/non-controllable and prior warning/no prior warning. Table 7.12 provides an example of a list of risks that can be adapted to fit into individual organizational contexts.

There are a number of approaches through which risk information can be collected across the organization and from its operating environment. In addition, the table below (Table 7.13) provides the key sources where additional risk information can be obtained.

Evaluation

This stage helps management to define where focus and resources should be invested. A realistic view should be adopted when assessing the probability of the risk. For instance, the probability of a fire outbreak is more likely in an oil refinery than in a soft drinks bottling plant. There is also a range of factors that could influence the

TABLE 7.12 Examples of natural and man-made risks

Natural	Man-Made	
• Extreme weather	• Supply chains	• Information security
• Flooding	• Power outages	• Physical security
• Climate change	• Human errors	• Facilities
• Earthquakes	• Fire and explosions	• Technologies
• Tidal surges	• Human resources	• Health and safety
	• Terrorism	• Corporate controls and systems failure
	• Pandemics	
	• Wilful acts	• Legal compliance
	• Business crimes	• Business and management

TABLE 7.13 Sources of information for risk identification

Sources of Information	Description
1. Workshops	• As part of the BIA information-gathering process • A follow-up workshop focusing on risks to critical activities
2. Interviews	• From risk management specialists within the organization • Details of specific risks from in-house 'experts', such as critical functions, processes and key suppliers
3. Documentary review	• Past reports of incidents in the organization • Past reports of incidents in the industry • Relevant reports about past incidents in related industries
4. External support	• Advice from public authorities • Relevant groups to share information and experiences pertaining to risks and management • External support to facilitate information-gathering sessions

probability of occurrence, such as human actions, geographical location and organizational culture.

After the probability of risks are established, the next step determines their impacts and ensuing consequences. An effective approach is to establish relationships between different risks that could affect the critical function – whether they are dependent or independent, that is, triggered by other risks or not. The loss potentials (impacts) could be compounded to reflect a more vivid picture of risks. In general, impacts are considered the immediate losses to business. In contrast, consequences mainly comprise intangible costs, which may give rise to long-term implications, such as reputational damage and loss of public confidence. The evaluation of these impacts should take into account the perspectives of the organization, customers and other key stakeholders. Once the profile of individual risks (probability and impact) has been established, the subsequent process is the calculation and ranking of risks. In most cases, the multiplication of probability and impact will provide a score for the risk. It should be stressed that the scores do not necessarily provide any absolute meaning; they only serve as a guide in making decisions on the identification of priorities.

Though this is a simple approach to risk management, the results should be used with care since the information can skew the interpretation of the risk. Taking a 5 × 5 scoring system, a risk scoring 25 (high probability with high impact) is most likely to prompt immediate attention for mitigation measures to prevent its occurrence. On the other hand, a risk with the score of 5 (low probability with high impact) may not command the same attention, and its significance is often downplayed. Given the low probability of these risks, developing costly mitigation measures may not provide a satisfactory return on investment. However, from the business continuity perspective, these are the risks that should call for the planning of business continuity and mitigation strategies.

Figure 7.1 provides a simple risk probability/impact chart with four options for the resilience programme.

FIGURE 7.1 Risk probability/impact chart and four options of resilience programmes

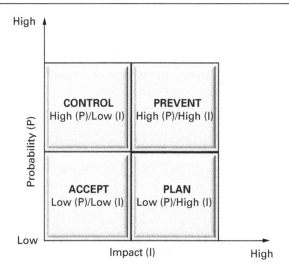

The four areas reflect the following attributes:

- Low probability/Low impact – Risks in this area are often negligible. In most cases, the decision is to accept them, though some measures could be devised to minimize the effects.

- Low probability/High impact – Risks are considered significant when they occur. The approach is to plan for the potential incidents in order to minimize the impact.

- High probability/Low impact – Risks occur frequently but often result in low consequences. The most common approach is to develop controls to minimize occurrence.

- High probability/High impact – Risks with high likelihood and devastating impacts should be prevented by all means possible.

Mitigation

In most cases, the selection of mitigation options for managing risks is dependent on the management capability of an organization. Primarily, there are four types of options that provide different levels of corporate protection:

- Accept – This option is based on the organization's risk appetite. It assumes that the known risks are marginal and can be easily overcome.

- Plan – This option looks into various forms of planning, chiefly, business continuity, risk, recovery and contingency. Given the low probability but high impact characteristics, planning to manage these risks when they occur can be a cost-effective business decision.

- Control – This option takes the approach of developing a regime of countermeasures to reduce or stop the risks that are occurring.

- Prevent – This option adopts the risk management principles of eliminating the risks through a series of preventive and control measures. The cost is justified by the high probability and impact nature of these risks.

The choice of approach is often influenced by organizational factors, such as the risk appetite, corporate resource capability and mitigation effects of the approach. It is most likely that organizations will adopt a combination of approaches to manage the four types of risk in the risk probability/impact chart.

Monitoring and review

Monitoring and review involves keeping track of the identified risks (including residual risks) and identifying emerging risks. It monitors trigger conditions for mitigation responses and constantly reviews the effectiveness of risk-mitigation strategies. As a crucial change driver in the RA process, it helps in making decisions on improving the risk management capability in advance of potential risks occurring. It is important that information from this stage is taken into account when reviewing the BCMS performance.

The purpose of monitoring and review is to determine the following:

- The validity of the planning assumptions for risk management
- Whether mitigation responses have been implemented as planned
- That processes and procedures are adhered to
- The effectiveness of mitigation responses through independent evaluations and testing or whether existing responses should be improved
- Changes in risks and their exposures or if new responses are required
- Areas of improvement in the risk assessment process

Risk assessment outputs

The RA findings form an integral part of the BIA report. It should include a prioritized list of risks to critical functions, profiling their individual characteristics and appropriate mitigation strategies to minimize their occurrence and impacts. In addition, those listed in Table 7.10 should be part of the risk outputs. The information is then used to guide the allocation of resources to treat those risks, both in terms of likelihood and consequences.

Strategy selection and development

Strategy selection and development focuses on the determination of the most appropriate operating arrangements to achieve the defined LBC of operation. In most cases, the breadth and depth of the chosen options and solutions are influenced by recovery requirements of critical functions, including urgency, complexity and resource types.

This stage consists of four elements:

1 Strategy options evaluation and selection

2 Process continuity responses

3 Consolidation of recovery resources

4 Strategy selection and development report

Strategy options evaluation and selection

The identification and selection of strategies should be based on the resource recovery requirements of critical function (see example in Table 7.9). This information helps to establish the criteria for evaluating the most appropriate option.

Though the time factor plays a vital part in the selection process, the following corporate factors should also be taken into consideration:

- Operational requirements – This refers to achieving the standard of service delivery in order to fulfil contractual and regulatory obligations.

- Cost – This is directly related to the speed of recovery. A shorter RTO accounts for a higher cost of implementation whilst a longer RTO tends to provide a cheaper option. The decision can be informed by a cost-benefit analysis, which assesses the operational and financial impact of the critical function versus the cost of implementing the recovery option.

- Recovery phases – Though it is important to address all phases of recovery – continuity (immediate phase), resumption (stabilization phase) and reinstatement (business-as-usual phase) – the management decision is often dependent on the criticality and impact of individual functions. In many cases, functions with significant impact require recovery options that can maintain a defined LBC to meet corporate and obligatory requirements. In contrast, those with lesser impact can adopt later phase options, such as repair and reinstatement.

In general, there are six approaches for developing BCM strategy options:

- Multi-site operation
- Backup arrangement
- Standby arrangement
- Third-party arrangement
- Modification
- Combined arrangement

Multi-site operation

The multi-site operation approach is suitable for organizations operating across a number of different sites where the critical products and services are delivered. The rationale is that having geographically dispersed locations minimizes the likelihood that sites will be affected by the same risk factors. If an incident renders a site unavailable, critical functions can be transferred to other locations to minimize impact to operations. Nonetheless, it is important to consider the operational capacity of the alternate sites in managing the extra workloads. This approach can also diversify the concentration of risks at particular locations.

Backup arrangement

The backup approach is characterized by the utilization of an appropriate secondary location to back up critical operations at the primary site. It adequately addresses two management concerns: the cost of implementing a BCM strategy, and corporate confidentiality about critical activities. In most cases, the effectiveness of this approach depends on the required calibrations and resource availability at the backup site to support the recovery process. Though its merits outweigh the demerits, a number of concerns must be reviewed, including how the activities are transferred to the alternate location and potential knock-on effects to the backup site's workforce and existing workload.

Standby arrangement

This arrangement is generally provided by specialist third parties. Though the agreement is catered to the organization's particular requirements, some configurations may still be necessary, such as vacant premises with basic utilities. This is suitable for critical functions with RTOs in hours rather than in minutes. Operations and logistical arrangements will require time to be re-established at a different location. This approach is likely to be the preferred choice for organizations operating in more than one site since they have the capability to accommodate additional operations on short notice. In addition, this arrangement addresses the issues of cost, corporate confidentiality and the reliability of third-party arrangement, if it is delivered internally.

Third-party arrangement

Third-party contractual recovery arrangement is about seeking external support in rebuilding the key processes that deliver the organization's products and services. This includes hiring equipment, such as office furniture, generators, telecommunications systems and standby buildings, to establish office-based operations. In order to expedite the recovery process, it is necessary to determine the requirements in advance of any unforeseen incident. This option is likely to be a primary strategy for organizations that operate in service and manufacturing, which are predominantly people-intensive. In certain cases, agency staff may be outsourced to support the recovery process. Although this might be an immediate solution, it is, in fact, a complex management challenge. Many issues will come to the fore, including skills and experiences, utilization and productivity rate, and obligations between the organization and third-party contractors.

Modification

Under certain circumstances, it may be necessary to modify the process of operation. The modification option is appropriate where there are limited resources to maintain the standard level of delivery following an incident. This calls for 'agile working', that is, bypassing some processes or reducing the level of operation in certain functions in order to reassign resources to more critical utilization. This can alleviate the immediate impact of the incident whilst expediting the recovery process. To ensure this option is feasible, it is important to undertake a thorough analysis of those standby functions. This ensures that the implementation of a reductionist strategy will not significantly affect other parts of operation. This option is very much influenced by the criticality of the standby functions, service peaks and troughs, backlog issues and other factors unique to the organization.

Combined arrangement

This option offers the flexibility and balances the strengths and weaknesses of the available options. Most organizations would prefer a combined strategy that could respond to a range of eventualities. It also helps to address key management concerns, such as the extent of planning, cost of implementation and contractual agreement between the organization and third-party suppliers.

Process continuity responses

Process continuity responses focus on the selection of continuity solutions for each critical function that supports the delivery of the organization's products and services. It is important that the continuity solution is based on the selected BCM strategy option.

When selecting a continuity solution, the following factors should be considered:

- Assumptions – The planning assumptions should always adopt the worst-case scenario in which the preferred solutions are implemented. This ensures that the assumptions are aligned with the probable risk events and all key resources are taken into account when planning.

- Procedures – The level of detail in the continuity solution is influenced by the complexity of the function to be recovered. Consideration should be given as to whether the procedures should be adhered to accordingly or if they can be adapted to meet the situation at hand.

- Requirements – The solution should address the organization's contractual and obligatory requirements. It should also take into account the potential implications of relevant laws and stakeholder expectations.

- Resources – Internal and external resources should be readily available to support the selected continuity solution. If specialized resources are required, they should be sourced and secured with the suppliers.

- Process – This refers to the key attributes of each continuity solution: its effectiveness of achieving the recovery timescales, how it is implemented, its interface with other internal and external processes, and the implications if it is delivered by a third-party contractor.

There are five key resources that should be made available to support the selected continuity solutions:

- People – Staff who undertake key organizational activities will need to be available. The emphasis is on those unique skills and expertise in making decisions and choosing actions that help to maintain the continuity of the organization's critical functions.

- Premises – In most cases, this is the predetermined accommodation based at a separate location. The location acts as a backup site for housing the critical functions in an incident that renders the primary site unavailable. Consideration should be given to the type of work area recovery arrangement, the length of time in which the alternate premises can be made ready, and staff willingness to travel to the new location.

- Information – This refers to vital records required by an organization to stay in operation. The backup and recovery regime, confidentiality and currency of the information should be factored into the process continuity response.

- Technologies – This refers to the technological infrastructures that support the recovery of critical business systems. It is important that these backup technologies and disaster recovery strategies are established and tested to ensure their adequacy in supporting the restoration process.

- Supplies – This refers to essential stocks, equipment and services that deal with various aspects of the recovery process. Where the critical function is dependent on specialist contractors and their services, it is important to establish strategies to secure their availability during an incident.

Table 7.14 summarizes the five forms of resources and their general considerations.

Consolidation of recovery resources

Recovery resources have a major influence on the selection of continuity solutions and are directly linked to the requirements defined in the BIA. This stage assesses the determined levels of resources required to implement the selected continuity solutions. It comprises four steps:

- Compile – Collate and validate all resource requirements of the selected continuity solutions, including those supported by third-party providers.

- Check – Compare and assess the requirements with the organization's current resource inventory list and the findings of the BCRRA. This ensures that the proposed demands are consistent with the current availability and there are no conflicts of requirements between the chosen solutions.

- Clarify and confirm – Clarify the requirements with business leads. In cases where there is a false confidence of resource information, it may be necessary to re-evaluate the BCM strategy options and continuity solutions.

- Commit – Once the resource requirements have been finalized, the information is prepared and recommended to the senior leadership team for approval. Their commitment will set in motion a series of projects for the development of BCM strategy options and continuity solutions.

TABLE 7.14 General considerations of key resources

Resources	Considerations
1. People	• Training: Establish structured training programmes and schemes to develop core skills amongst a wider group of staff who are currently supporting the delivery of critical products and services.
	• Diversification: This is a risk-based approach that minimizes the concentration of risks to the organization's critical workforce. Strategies include different work locations for key staff and separate travel arrangement plans.
	• Documentation: Develop a knowledge management system that records how critical skills and activities are performed. Consideration should also be given to the level of knowledge and experience required to undertake the tasks.
	• Succession planning: The nomination of individuals to back up key staff. This is often in the form of mentorship or deputies. This method can be underpinned by training arrangements.
	• Specialist third parties: The engagement of specialist contractors to undertake the organization's critical activities. Though it provides some level of assurance to the continuity of operation, it does not address organizational 'soft' issues, such as corporate culture, client relationships, business strategies and corporate confidentiality.
2. Premises	• Secondary location: An alternate work location designated to house the critical operations when the primary site becomes unavailable. This arrangement can be delivered internally or supported by third-party providers.
	• Third-party providers: The use of alternative workplaces provided by specialist contractors. This is regulated by the terms and conditions stipulated in the contract. Availability upon notification, recovery timescales of critical operations, distance and staff travel, and business requirements unique to the organization should be taken into account.
	• Flexible working arrangement: This is a temporary arrangement of working in designated locations, such as business centres, client offices and home.
	• Reciprocal arrangement: An agreement between two or more organizations to use each other's premises and facilities in the event of an incident.

(Continued)

TABLE 7.14 *(Continued)*

Resources	Considerations
3. Information	• Backup and recovery: The backup methods for information and how effective the recovery processes are. • Confidentiality: The sensitivity of the critical products and services (and their activities) should be adequately safeguarded. • Availability: The formats in which the information is recorded – paper or electronic – and the storage media in which they are kept. • Completeness: This refers to the integrity of information in terms of accuracy and reliability. • Currency: This is vital in the recovery of key operations. Currency refers to the information required to support the continuity of critical activities. In order to achieve an effective recovery, the information needs to be complete and acceptably up-to-date. This is influenced by the backup and recovery regime.
4. Technologies	• Power: Determine the requirements necessary to provide an uninterrupted power system (UPS) for the primary and backup data centres and critical infrastructures. Consideration should also be given to the duration and reliability of the UPS. In addition, there should be standard procedures to acquire, install, test and maintain such a system. • Network: Determine the requirements for voice and data communications, and network connection. This information will establish the network system in the backup data centre. It is also important to consider adopting a diversity of connectivity technology to enhance performance and minimize single points of failure. • Backup storage: Generally storage includes hard/portable disks, magnetic tapes, optical storages, solid state storages and remote backup services. Factors to consider include security, portability, compatibility, reliability, and backup and technical requirements. • Systems software: Backup copies of software applications should be maintained at an alternate site. It is important to test the integration between hardware and software, and verify that the systems are performing as expected at the secondary location.

(Continued)

TABLE 7.14 (*Continued*)

Resources	Considerations
	• Hardware: Consider backup, repair, replace or temporary loan options for critical hardware and equipment damaged during an incident. Determine business and technical requirements, such as cost, specifications, age and compatibility with existing hardware and software systems. • Backup data centre: This is an integral part of the organization's BCM strategy option. Space requirements and technical specifications should be considered as part of the continuity planning process.
5. Supplies	• Buffer stocks: Additional supplies are stocked for emergencies. These can be stockpiled in warehouses or any secured location. • Contractual agreements: Arrangements with third-party suppliers to deliver critical stocks on short notice. In many cases, this arrangement is reinforced by legal terms and penalties. • Alternative sourcing: A wide selection of critical suppliers to secure timely delivery of supplies. • Validation of business continuity arrangements: An imposed requirement to all existing and potential suppliers to demonstrate their business continuity capability – business continuity plans validated by exercises or audit reports. This ensures resilience in the supply chain network. • Diversification: Develop a broad base of critical suppliers from different sources. This assures their critical services and supplies are not compromised during unforeseen incidents.

Strategy selection and development report

At the minimum, a complete strategy selection and development report should include the following items:

- A list of BCM strategy options – This sets out the high-level BCM strategy for each critical function. Each selected option should address the management concerns in terms of business requirements, cost of implementation and how the option achieves the recovery objectives. This should be supported by a cost-benefit analysis.

- A list of feasible continuity solutions – The continuity solutions are established based on the selected BCM strategy options. The solutions can be grouped according to critical functions to which they are related, such as types of activity and recovery time objectives.

- Description of each solution – The features of each continuity solution should include operating costs, terms and conditions, extent of planning, resource availability, implementation timescale and adaptability to support other critical functions.

- Operational considerations – This includes the operating assumptions and limitations of each continuity solution – its strengths and weaknesses in terms of effectiveness, applications and performance under certain conditions.

- Project management – This covers the project management aspects of the BCM strategy development, that is, how the continuity solution is developed and established – the duration, defined tasks, resources required (where and how to secure them) and the deliverables.

Establish business continuity capability

As a key component of the business continuity capability, the incident management structure (IMS) implements the necessary command and control to ensure that the incident management process proceeds appropriately during an incident.

It comprises different management groups spanning from members of the senior leadership team to supporting staff of critical functions. Individual management groups are responsible for different types of incident and may be required to escalate the incident if it goes beyond the group's management capacity. As such, different levels of incident management plans (IMPs) are developed to enable individual groups within the IMS to fulfil their given tasks.

Incident management structure

The incident management structure (IMS) is an approach for commanding, controlling and coordinating the recovery efforts of individual teams within the organization. The teams work towards the common goal of containing the incident – protecting lives, corporate assets and the environment.

In the broadest sense, the IMS comprises three types of teams, which focus on different levels of management activities: strategic, tactical and operational. Depending on the scale and complexity of the organization, the IMS can be adapted to fit into the organizational context. For instance, for organizations with a leaner structure, a two-tier approach is often adopted, that is, the strategic and tactical teams are merged and provide direction to the operational team.

- Strategic – The strategic team consists of strategic decision-makers and staff at the group level. They establish the overarching framework and its policy guidelines that the tactical and operational teams operate in incident management. In addition, the team addresses the wider long-term implications of the incident on the affected business areas. Predominantly, it focuses on preserving the corporate reputation and communicating with the media. It also bolsters the tactical and operational teams by providing the necessary resources for managing the incident.

- Tactical – The tactical team is responsible for determining how the impact of the incident is managed within the policy guidelines set by the strategic team. The team would consider issues directly surrounding the incident, such as access to the affected premises and transfer of critical operations to alternate locations. It also assumes the crucial role of facilitating activities between the strategic and operational teams. Depending on the nature of the incident, there may be specific groups dealing with key aspects of the incident response, such as facilities management, communication, staff welfare and emergency coordination.

- Operational – The general functions of the operational team include implementing recovery strategies based on the decisions made by the strategic and tactical teams. Further operational subteams may be established to focus on specific issues of the incident, such as business recovery, information technology disaster recovery and site security.

In order to foster effective communication amongst the different management groups, there should be coordinators for regulating information and its flow. Their key responsibilities are as follows:

- Validate information – Check and ensure the reliability of information prior to dissemination.

- Communicate information – The timely dissemination of information for making decisions and carrying out actions.

- Act as the point of liaison between the teams – Act as the single source of contact in order to control the flow of information.

- Attend meetings – This establishes a clear knowledge of the decisions made or actions taken in order to disseminate the updates to the relevant teams.

Figure 7.2 illustrates the IMS and its key components

FIGURE 7.2 Incident management structure

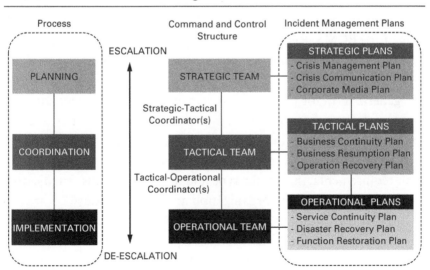

Command and control

In order to establish an effective incident response, the IMS should be appropriately organized based on three key aspects:

1 Information – This refers to the type and nature of information required by the teams in managing the incident. There should be controls to regulate the dissemination of sensitive information in the communication process.

2 Activities and actions – This is primarily influenced by the roles and responsibilities of the management team. In most cases, the strategic team defines the incident management objectives, priorities and strategies whilst the operational team, supported by the tactical team, implements the recovery strategies to achieve the set objectives.

3 Control – This refers to the degree of autonomy in the incident management process. This includes the authority and type of decisions each team is capable of exercising in performing the tasks.

Table 7.15 summarizes the key characteristics of the three management functions.

Incident management plans

The incident management plans (IMPs) are one of the ultimate products of the BCMS. Regardless of their purpose and level of detail, the plans are documents that contain processes and procedures ready to be implemented following an incident. It is worth noting that 'IMPs' is a general term for plans used in managing incidents. Depending on their level of application, they can be known by other titles, such as 'crisis management plan' (CMP), 'business continuity plans' (BCPs) or 'function restoration plans' (FSPs) (Figure 7.2). In most cases, the plan requirements, that is, the type and number of plans, are dictated by the complexity of the organization and its operations.

In large organizations that are geographically dispersed, it would be practical to have different levels of plans as separate documents to manage a range of incidents. Each plan has a specific purpose,

TABLE 7.15 Characteristics of incident management structure

	Levels of Incident Management Structure (IMS)		
	Strategic	**Tactical**	**Operational**
Role	• Oversight	• Supervision	• Execution
Responsibilities	• Receive and assess information from the tactical team about the impact of the incident on the critical operations • Decide on appropriate strategies to deal with the incident and its impact	• Determine recovery responses required to manage the immediate impact of an incident – factors affecting people, premises/facilities and critical infrastructures • Decide, act and communicate within the strategic parameters set by the strategic team • Provide information to the strategic team about the status of the incident or effects of the recovery responses taken • Implement any actions advised by the emergency services • Provide advice and instructions to operational team members pertaining to the actions required to manage the incident • Monitor the progress of the incident • Escalate key issues that arise from the incident	• Implement recovery responses in their areas of operation • Act upon decisions and strategies of the strategic and tactical teams • Decide, act and communicate within the strategic parameters set by the strategic team • Provide information to the tactical team about the status of the incident or effects of the recovery responses taken • Implement any actions advised by the emergency services • Monitor the progress of the incident • Escalate key issues that arise from the incident

(Continued)

TABLE 7.15 (Continued)

	Levels of Incident Management Structure (IMS)		
	Strategic	**Tactical**	**Operational**
Composition	• Chief Executive, Business Continuity Director, Facilities Director or their equivalents, Directors (critical functions) and other roles of strategic importance	• Business heads, senior managers (Business Continuity and Facilities or their equivalents), senior managers (critical functions) and staff with oversight responsibilities at business level	• Functional managers, supervisory staff (critical functions), specialist staff and nominated staff
Considerations	• BCM strategy options for critical functions if the primary location becomes unavailable • Working arrangements for staff if premises become unavailable (e.g. alternate locations or work from home)	• Accountability for and welfare of staff and stakeholders affected by the incident. Identify any casualties and liaise with emergency services about their care • Transfer of critical operations and resources to alternate locations • Communication with local stakeholders (internal and external) about the incident and the organization's response to it • Approval from strategic team of information prior to dissemination	• Guidance from appropriate teams if significant issues arise from implementing the decisions and responses • Measures to ensure the safety and security of affected premises until the incident is over and they are subsequently re-occupied • Operational impacts • Roles of tactical-operational coordinators

(Continued)

TABLE 7.15 (*Continued*)

Levels of Incident Management Structure (IMS)		
Strategic	**Tactical**	**Operational**
• Communication with the media and strategic stakeholders about the incident and the organization's response to it • Conveyance of external messages • Necessary actions to protect the organization's reputation • Organization's liabilities and obligations due to delivery failure • Operational, financial and non-financial impacts • Roles of strategic-tactical coordinators	• Recovery timeframes of critical functions as established by those organizational functions that have operational responsibility for them • Operational and financial impacts • Roles of strategic-tactical/tactical-operational coordinators	
Process		
• Planning	• Coordination	• Implementation
Level of Control		
• Head Office	• Regional	• Local
Scope		
• Crisis Management	• Business Continuity Management	• Emergency/Recovery/Salvage Management

which could be used in isolation under certain circumstances. On the other hand, for small to medium organizations, it is more practical to address issues arising from the incident with a single document.

When designing the organization's IMPs, a good starting point would be to adopt the structure illustrated in Figure 7.2.

- Strategic plan – This plan provides high-level guidance to enable directors and executives to manage the strategic nature of an incident. It comprises strategies that address impacts to the organization's 'soft' assets, such as corporate reputation, shareholder confidence and long-term performance of the business.

- Tactical plan – This plan sets out the framework of actions to be taken at business level in response to an incident affecting the critical functions. It consists of a number of solutions for managing the continuity of key operations. The tactical plan facilitates cooperation with operational teams since the selected options form the basis for responses at the operational level.

- Operational plan – This plan comprises details of business continuity procedures of critical functions. It addresses operational issues from the outbreak of an incident to the point at which acceptable LBC is achieved.

Key elements of IMPs

Managing incidents can be a perplexing experience since the responsibilities for sustaining the organization's reputation and critical operations during abnormal situations are shouldered by a handful of nominated staff. One of the key functions of IMPs is to minimize the time for decision-making. In order to ensure plans are fit-for-purpose, they should be designed with the following principles:

- Adaptable – The plans should be capable of responding to a range of incidents, anticipated and unanticipated.

- Concise – The plan should contain only relevant information that helps to mitigate the impact of the incident as well as expedite the recovery process.

- Targets – These are expressed in terms of milestones and outcomes. They are essential to monitoring the recovery progress and adequacy of BCM strategies and procedures.

- Comprehensible – The language of instructions should be simple and clear. The use of checklists and diagrams can enhance the usability of the plan.

- Sequential – Sections of the plan should be progressive and readily identifiable. This helps to develop an initial understanding of the incident before activating the appropriate responses. For instance, sections on the scope and objectives of the plan should come before items such as team invocation and response processes.

- Consistent – The plans should conform to a standard format appropriate to the organization. This ensures that those who are transferred from another location can readily understand and assume their nominated roles during an incident.

Although the plan content differs between organizations, there are a number of key elements that should be considered during the plan development stage. They are broadly grouped into two components: front matters and back matters. The former addresses the immediate situation following an incident. The latter contains pertinent information about the organization and staff that helps the team to manage an incident more effectively.

Front matters

- Document information – The title of the corporate function and details of document control
- Content – Section headings with respective page numbers
- Diagram/Checklist – The graphical format of the incident management process. Alternatively, this can be a checklist of activities
- Scope – The scales and types of incident covered by the plan
- Objectives – The desired outcomes of the plan
- Limitations – A list of conditions for which the plan does not apply

- Decision criteria – An agreed upon definition of an incident or a checklist of threshold criteria to guide the decision for declaring an incident, such as 50% of the staff becoming unavailable

- Invocation procedures – The invocation protocol that states who is responsible for invoking the plan. This also includes the process and procedures of team mobilization

- Escalation procedures – The organization's IMS, which explains who is responsible for alerting the next higher level of management if the incident goes beyond the scope of the plan

- Communication process – The protocol of communicating information between various teams and external agencies

- Action lists – A brief information about individual critical products and services (and dependencies, if relevant) supported by a set of defined actions to achieve the recovery timescales

Back matters

- IMS chart – The graphical format that illustrates the relationship and interface between different management groups

- Roles and responsibilities – Defined roles and responsibilities of teams and individuals in the incident management process

- Contact list – A list of contact details of key stakeholders

- Incident command centre (ICC) – The process and procedures for setting up the ICC

- Log sheet – A recording form that documents the process of managing the incident

- Demobilization procedures – The standing down process of incident management teams

- References – The relationship between the plan and other organizational plans and policies

Table 7.16 outlines the key items of an IMP and their points of consideration.

TABLE 7.16 Key items of IMP and points of consideration

Items	Considerations

Document information	• Title of the corporate function.
	• Month and year of the approved plan.
	• Document control should include the following:
	  – Copy number
	  – Version number
	  – Issue date
	  – Issue to

Content	• Text style and size should be consistently applied throughout the plan. • Key section headings and page numbers should be readily identifiable. • Section headings should be short and concise. • Section headings and page numbers in the main document should correspond to their respective sections and page numbers in the content page.
Scope	• Incident types should be broadly classified into probable scenarios that will lead to the loss of functions. • Scope should not be overly specific; otherwise, the plan will be limited and narrowly restricted.

Objectives	• Objectives should be expressed in statements.
	• They should have the following characteristics:
	  – Clear and concise
	  – Realistic
	  – Capable of being evaluated

Limitations	• Develop a list of scenarios that the incident management procedures do not address. • Limitations should be related to the scope of the plan.
Decision criteria	• Use a process flow diagram to guide the incident assessment process. • Label the diagram well. • Incorporate prompt questions in the diagram to guide the decision-making process or what actions to adopt. • Define what an incident is. • Alternatively, use a threshold criteria to define an incident.

(Continued)

TABLE 7.16 (*Continued*)

Items	Considerations
Invocation process	• Use a process flow diagram to illustrate the invocation process. • Define the means of informing the team members. • Define the time required to mobilize the team. • Use predetermined 'code-word' to declare the incident. This helps to minimize miscommunication and confusion. • Determine the primary and secondary assembly locations.
Escalation procedures	• Define the criteria and means of escalation. • Determine who is responsible for escalating the incident.

Communication process	• Use a process flow diagram to illustrate the communication process.
	• Develop a list of internal and external stakeholders and their contact details.
	• Identify the external agencies that will be required to support the incident management process.
	• The following elements should be included when developing the communication strategies:
	  – Who – the target groups of stakeholders
	  – What – the content of the information
	  – When – the timing of dissemination
	  – How – the means of communication

Action lists	• Include corporate charts – key diagrams to show how various functions and activities relate to one another and make up the organizational process. • Use a process flow diagram to illustrate the delivery process for each critical product and service (including its dependencies). • Incorporate recovery timelines in the diagram. • Recovery activities should be based on priorities of operation – determined by the BIA. • Recovery activities should be sequential or in parallel, based on an approved recovery timeline of activities. • Produce a list of resources required to support the recovery process along with where and how to acquire them.

(*Continued*)

TABLE 7.16 *(Continued)*

Items	Considerations
IMS chart	• Use a diagram to illustrate the relationship between different management groups (see Figure 7.2). • Provide an overview of each management group.
Roles and responsibilities	• Define the objectives of each team and individual. • Roles and responsibilities should be concise and not overlapping. • A deputy should be assigned to each key role. • Use RACI – responsible, accountable, consulted and informed, if necessary. • Produce a description of the roles and responsibilities of emergency services during a major incident.
Contact list	• Produce a list of primary and secondary contact details.
Incident command centre (ICC)	• Define the primary and secondary locations. • Include contact details of venue providers. • Provide a checklist of activities for setting up the ICC. • Provide a checklist of items required in the ICC for the following: 　– Communication – the receipt and dissemination of information and instructions 　– Security – controlled access to the location 　– Administration – the analysis, recording and management of information in support of the incident management process 　– Management – the monitoring and management of the incident 　– Staff welfare – the access to refreshments, resting areas, toilets and washing facilities • Provide the location of the grab bag. • At the minimum, the contents of the grab bag should include the following: 　– Mobile phones (stored with key contacts) and chargers 　– Contact list of key individuals 　– IMPs (paper version)

(Continued)

TABLE 7.16 (Continued)

Items	Considerations

Log sheet	• Key components include the following:
	  – Incident type
	  – Date
	  – Sequence number
	  – Time logged
	  – Description (for decisions made, actions taken and information received)
	  – Name of log keeper
	  – Signature

Demobilization procedures	• Develop a checklist to ensure that various aspects of the incident have been contained before standing down the teams.
References	• Use a diagram to illustrate how the plan relates to key organizational plans and policies. • Provide a high-level summary of each plan and policy.

A project management approach can be adopted when developing the organization's IMP template. In most cases, the plan template is developed by the central BCM team, which then provides support to the organizational functions in completing their plans. The following diagram (Figure 7.3) illustrates a typical plan development process.

Exercise business continuity capability

Exercises are an essential element of the BCMS. No matter how comprehensive a BCP may be or how well-designed the procedures are, the plan is not considered complete until it has been validated by a series of realistic exercises. Exercising is a critical driver in the maintenance of plans; it ensures that they will work during an incident. Though the challenges presented by every incident are different,

FIGURE 7.3 Plan development process

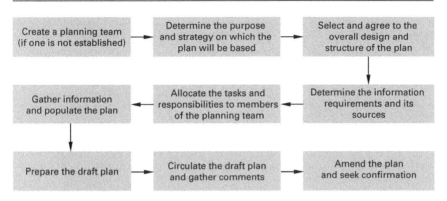

plans that are exercised have a much higher possibility of succeeding than those that have never been validated.

An exercise will uncover areas for improvement. It rehearses roles and responsibilities of team members whilst evaluating the appropriateness of strategies and procedures in the BCP. An exercise should be seen as an opportunity to assess the quality of planning, to train individual business continuity capability, and to ensure that technical, logistical and administrative activities are collectively integrated in a real situation.

It is worth noting that the term 'test' is primarily concerned in assessing two possibilities – passing and failing – and is generally applied in the field of disaster recovery. As such, the term should not be applied to staff since they do not want the outcome of their actions to be judged as 'pass' or 'fail' (alternatively 'right' or 'wrong'). Though testing is a narrow approach to assessment, it forms an integral element of the BCM exercise programme.

Elements of exercising

Every form of exercise should set out its purpose, which should address one or more of the following principles:

- Demonstrating the plan is realistic and capable of working in the specified scenario
- Determining the actual length of recovery timescales

- Familiarizing and training staff for their designated BCM roles and responsibilities

- Ensuring all required resources are available to support the BCM strategies and arrangements

- Identifying areas of unknown contingency

- Raising the awareness of staff and stakeholders of the actions required by them in the plan

- Demonstrating that time and resources invested in exercising will lead to an adequate business continuity capability

Based on the seven principles, a number of requirements can be developed to assess the key aspects of the plan and team:

- Skills – How are their communicating and decision-making skills? Are the appointed individuals familiar with their responsibilities? Are they aware of the key actions required to complete the tasks in the plan?

- Technical – Do the equipment, systems and infrastructures work according to specifications?

- Procedures – Do the guidelines for performing the actions lead to the desired outcomes? Are they comprehensible to the team members?

- Logistical – Are the key resources and suppliers available as stated in the plan? Are details about the resources, equipment and inventories accurate? Do they support the BCM strategies and arrangements?

- Timelines: Are the recovery timescales realistic? Are the recovery timescales of dependencies taken into consideration?

Types of exercise

When the exercise format is designed, the level must be appropriate to the current state of the organization's BCMS, whilst taking into account the maturity of the BCM team. The most effective method is to adopt an incremental approach, which selects an exercise format that is compatible with the participants' knowledge and skills of the subject matter – for instance, running an orientation session or a desktop exercise before progressing to a functional exercise. In addition, it is important to note that realism is an essential feature of any exercise. This ensures that the scenario is credible and relevant. However, as the level (scale and complexity) progresses, the risk of disruption also increases. As such, those responsible for planning the event should ensure that such risks are made known to executive management. Appropriate risk measures should also be in place to abort the exercise if disruption becomes imminent.

In the broadest sense, exercising can be discussion-based or operation-based. Discussion-based exercises typically focus on the decision-making process and implications of the decisions taken. They familiarize participants with existing strategies in the plan whilst establishing the necessary knowledge and confidence. In contrast, operation-based exercises validate various aspects of the plan, namely, skills, technical aspects, procedures, logistical and timelines. They provide the opportunity for teams and plans to interface in a realistic scenario. They develop the necessary competence of individual participants as well as identifying areas for improvement in plans and procedures.

Figure 7.4 illustrates the exercise curve and the five levels of exercise as the BCM programme matures.

FIGURE 7.4 Five levels of exercise

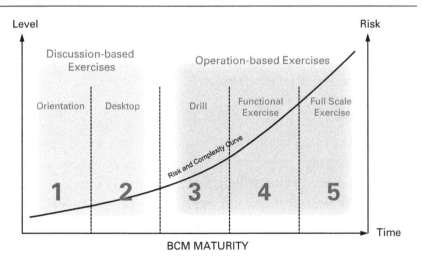

Exercises fall into the following five categories:

- Orientation
- Desktop
- Drill
- Functional exercise
- Full-scale exercise

Orientation

An orientation is a seminar-type activity that is conducted in an interactive and informal setting. Its key objective is to familiarize team members with the BCP and its procedures. This form of exercise is particularly suitable when there are new staff joining the team or when new procedures are added to the plan. Orientation activities include briefing on key aspects of the BCP, group and individual trainings, and discussion about the implementation of strategies.

Desktop

Desktop exercise is a discussion-based exercise in an informal setting. It involves senior managers and key personnel of critical functions in breakout groups, who discuss their roles and responsibilities in a hypothetical scenario. In most cases, it focuses on stimulating discussion about how participants would react to a specific BCM-related situation whilst identifying shortfalls in existing BCP procedures. Typical issues under discussion include the decision-making process, notification and assignment of roles and responsibilities. The exercise typically features an opening session, one or more plenary sessions and a post-exercise review session.

Drill

A drill is used to assess the recovery responses of a specific process in the function. This is typically an operation-based exercise that validates procedures in the BCP. It provides the opportunity for team members to acquire hands-on experience. This form of exercise requires good planning, coordination and control in order to minimize disruption to organizational operation.

Functional exercise

A functional exercise simulates a business continuity situation by presenting complex problems to key members of the team that require them to make decisions and take necessary actions to contain the impact. The purpose of this form of exercise is to review the adequacy of BCM strategies, individual capabilities and the collective effort of the function or a group of functions.

Full-scale exercise

A full-scale exercise is designed around a realistic scenario. It is the most complex and comprehensive form of exercise and places participants in circumstances resembling those of an actual incident. The setting can be stressful and time-based. The central tenet of this form of exercise is to validate all aspects of the organization's business continuity preparedness. It typically involves implementing actual processes used in a real incident, such as relocating to an alternate location and continuing the operation of critical functions using the available resources. In most cases, members of the exercise control inject additional scenario-based events at appropriate times to assess the participants' reactions. This presents challenging problems that call for critical thinking, rapid problem solving and effective responses.

Good quality exercises depend on realistic scenarios that will uncover areas for attention. It is important that an organization's exercise programme be progressive in terms of scale and complexity, beginning with discussion-based activities and escalating gradually to operation-based exercises.

Table 7.17 summarizes the key characteristics of the different exercises.

Exercise planning team

The most critical factor for a successful exercise is organizing a capable and experienced exercise planning team. This team has two primary functions: coordination and control. The team designs and manages all stages of the exercise activities: planning, delivery and post-administration. It ensures that participants and logistical

TABLE 7.17 Key characteristics of exercises

Types	Description	Purpose	Format	Duration	Frequency
Orientation	A workshop or seminar that briefs participants on their BCM roles and responsibilities	• Introduce newly assigned staff with the basic concepts of BCM (plans, procedures, roles and responsibilities) • Brief the concepts of different exercises and their challenges	• Presentations led by subject matter experts • Group discussions	1–3 hours	3–6 months
Desktop	A conference-style setting designed to foster discussion for identifying gaps in plans and individual skills	• Identify gaps in processes and participant capabilities • Familiarize participants with roles and responsibilities in the BCM process • Establish confidence and knowledge for the next level of exercise	• Narrative scenario or situation • Facilitated discussions • Discussion led by simulated scenarios/injects	3–6 hours	6–12 months

(Continued)

TABLE 7.17 (*Continued*)

Types	Description	Purpose	Format	Duration	Frequency
Drill	A controlled and supervised event that validates plans and recovery capability of staff in a single function/work location	• Assess the business continuity preparedness of individual functions • Provide participants with hands-on training and experience • Validate the effectiveness of interaction between teams and plans	• Realistic setting that takes place at the work location • Actual mobilization of certain resources • Typical activities include fire drills, building evacuations, and team activation and notification	30 minutes–2 hours	6–12 months
Functional exercise	A larger version of a drill that validates plans and recovery capability of staff in a collection of functions/work locations that contribute to the delivery of one or more critical products or services	• Assess the collective business continuity preparedness of a group of related functions • Acquire confidence and competence prior to undertaking a full-scale exercise • Validate the effectiveness of interaction between teams and plans	• Realistic setting simulating actual scenarios or complex field activities • Actions take place in real time and generate 'actual' consequences • Simulates business continuity situations without actual mobilizing of resources to alternate location(s)	3–8 hours (depends on the RTOs of functions under assessment)	12 months

(*Continued*)

TABLE 7.17 (Continued)

Types	Description	Purpose	Format	Duration	Frequency
Full-scale exercise	A complex event that intends to simulate a real situation in order to assess all aspects of the preparedness of an organization or its functions	• Evaluate all aspects of the teams and plans in a realistic scenario • Validate the effectiveness of interaction between teams and plans	• Realistic setting with actual mobilization of resources, which involves the integration of people, premises, operations, supplies and technologies • Involves the relocation of operations to one or more locations • As much as possible, participants are put under circumstances resembling actual incidents – BCP invocation, staff notification, relocation and operation at alternate locations • Interactive and complex – participants respond to a set of 'real' challenges	3–8 hours (it is usually a full-day event and also depends on the RTOs of functions and complexity of the recovery process)	12–18 months

and administrative supports come together as planned. In addition, the team oversees the whole exercise programme and corrects any issues that seem to deviate from the intended objective.

The key roles in the team usually include the following:

- Facilitator
- Controller
- Evaluator
- Participants
- Recorder
- Timekeeper
- Observers

Facilitator

In most cases, the facilitator has an active role in discussion-based exercises. This role assumes the responsibility for ensuring that participant discussion remains focused on the exercise agenda. The facilitator, who can be a BCM subject expert, has overall knowledge about the organization. The individual often directs and controls the pace of the exercise discussion. Key responsibilities of the facilitator include the following:

- Providing participants with the necessary information prior to the commencement of the exercise
- Providing exercise oversight, including supervising the exercise, monitoring the sequence of events and controlling the timeline
- Controlling and managing all activities during the exercise but not providing solutions during the discussion
- Conducting debrief or feedback sessions with participants following the exercise
- Making decisions in case of unforeseen circumstances during the exercise
- Leading the analysis of exercise information and assisting in the preparation of the post-exercise report to capture key lessons learned

Controller

The controller acts as an extension of the facilitator. The individual provides support to the facilitator during the exercise, including introducing injects at the instruction of the facilitator. This role also observes the participants during the exercise and ensures that they stay focused on the assigned tasks. Depending on the type of exercise, this role is often called 'facilitator' rather than 'controller' for discussion-based exercises. The controller tends to assume a larger role in operation-based exercises, which includes maintaining order as well as providing direction to the participants.

Evaluator

The evaluator usually takes a passive role and is not involved directly in the exercise. The individual's responsibilities include supporting the facilitator, recording decisions and actions, and identifying key issues raised during the exercise.

Participants

The participants are the members of the organization being assessed. They are usually members of the response teams who have designated roles and responsibilities in an actual incident. They are players in the exercise and are required to respond to the simulated events.

Recorder

The recorder is primarily responsible for recording information during discussion-based exercises. An integral part of the role is to provide support to the facilitator and the evaluator. Other tasks include disseminating exercise communication forms between team tables, note-taking and assisting in the creation of the post-exercise report.

Timekeeper

The timekeeper keeps track of the time during the administration of the discussion-based exercises. The individual works closely with the facilitator to ensure that time limits of exercise activities are adhered to.

Observers

This includes internal and external representatives of other functions within the organization, client organizations, suppliers and government agencies. They usually watch the entire or part of the exercise, and do not participate in any exercise activity. They note participants' performance and later report on their observations. Their comments are useful in capturing the entire exercise experience. Their key roles include participating in critiques and highlighting pertinent issues to the facilitator.

Table 7.18 illustrates the individual roles in different types of exercise.

Though the roles and responsibilities should be clearly defined and assigned to appropriate individuals, it is worth noting that they should not be rigidly applied since the number of staffing roles to support the exercise is often dictated by its type and complexity; it may be practical to merge or extend certain responsibilities to ensure that the required tasks are effectively carried out.

The exercise programme

The exercise programme is at the heart of the exercise process. It establishes the approach to achieving the exercise objectives. As such, the principles of developing an exercise programme should follow a structured process. Figure 7.5 illustrates the key stages of establishing an exercise programme, which are as follows:

Develop – Develop exercise objectives and scope

The development stage is about defining the purpose of exercising. It determines the exercise objectives and scope, and selects the most appropriate type of exercise to achieve the defined outcomes:

- Objectives should be developed with reference to the corporate business continuity policy and approved by the business continuity champion.
- The scope sets the scene of the exercise and describes what it intends to cover. It is important that the scope relates back to the exercise objectives.
- Identify the possible choices of exercise.

TABLE 7.18 Participation of individual roles in different levels of exercise

Exercises	Facilitator(s)	Controller(s)	Evaluator(s)	Participants	Recorder(s)	Timekeeper(s)	Observer(s)
Level 1	✓		✓	✓	✓		✓
Level 2	✓		✓	✓	✓	✓	✓
Level 3	✓		✓	✓			✓
Level 4	✓	✓	✓	✓			✓
Level 5	✓	✓	✓	✓			✓

Level 1: Orientation
Level 2: Desktop
Level 3: Drill
Level 4: Functional Exercise
Level 5: Full-Scale Exercise

FIGURE 7.5 Key stages of exercise programme

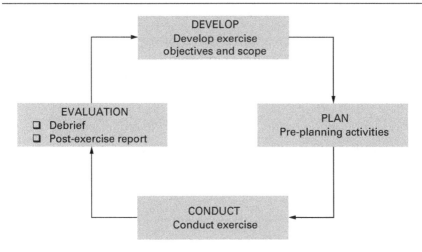

- The level (scale and complexity) of the exercise should take into consideration the maturity of the organization's BCMS.

- Develop a scorecard to assess the objectives. This can be in the form of criteria that measure the exercise success and whether the outcomes have been met.

- It is important that the exercise does not pose risk to the organization and its critical operations.

Plan – Pre-planning activities

The planning stage is the bulk of the exercise development and delivery. It sets out the key activities leading to the actual event. This is considered the most important stage of the entire exercise process since achievement of the exercise outcomes depends on the quality of planning. As such, it will inevitably consume many work hours in the preparation. In essence, it comprises team, administration, logistics, participants and communication.

- Team: This refers to the formation of the exercise planning team. It includes appointing the appropriate individuals with suitable skills and experiences.

  - Identify and organize the planning team.

- – Assign roles and responsibilities to team members.
- – Develop a schedule of pre-exercise activities.
- – Establish timelines and monitor the development process.

- Administration: This refers to the preparation of all key aspects of the pre-exercise event.

    i Exercise cost estimation and selection

    - – Use cost-benefit analysis to evaluate the choices of exercise. Orientation, desktop and drill tend to be lower-cost options.
    - – Identify the required resources and their costs to support the exercise option.
    - – Present in visual format the time and costs of running different exercise options to the business continuity champion and executive management.

    ii Agenda

    - – Provide the date, time and location of the exercise event.
    - – Include the specific timeframe for each exercise activity.
    - – Note who is responsible for each exercise activity.

    iii Exercise materials

    - – Select a probable scenario that would trigger the activation of the BCP.
    - – Ensure the type of injects is of suitable style to match the exercise purpose and the competence of participants.
    - – Separate the injects into different phases: plan activation, incident response, business continuity and recovery and business-as-usual.
    - – Provide detailed information for each inject – what has happened so far: time, damage status, staff and other information pertaining to the incident.
    - – If necessary, develop 'dummy' materials such as notes, news reports and documentary evidence to add realism.

- Include interruptions to control the exercise. These should be used if participants' focus has drifted (particularly in discussion-based exercises).

- Develop risk controls to halt the exercise if circumstances pose threats to the organization and its activities (particularly in operation-based exercises).

iv Exercise concept plan

- The plan is intended to provide participants with information prior to the exercise event.

- The plan should include objectives and scope, participants, exercise format, topics and references to be reviewed prior to the exercise.

- Rules of engagement could also be included to state the dos and don'ts, and what resources are available during the exercise.

v Evaluation plan

- This plan is developed based on the approved exercise objectives.

- Define what needs to be assessed in each inject.

- At the minimum, the plan should cover the following:

  - Items to be evaluated – plan procedures, team/individual capability (in terms of skills, knowledge and behaviours) and team-plan interface

  - Evaluation techniques – observation or questioning

  - Who is responsible for undertaking the evaluation

  - Measures of effectiveness – the objective criteria for assessing the exercise

vi General

- Collect and review related policies, plans and reports for the exercise.

- Use a checklist to ensure that key activities and tasks have been completed.

- Develop and coordinate schedules for the planning team, internal exercise participants and external participating partners and agencies.

- Schedule planning meetings.

- Participants: This refers to the identification of players who have roles and responsibilities in the organization's BCMS. It is also important to select and involve external exercise participants, particularly those who support the delivery of the organization's critical products and services.

- Logistics: This refers to the venue, facilities and other miscellaneous arrangements that support the running of the exercise.

  - Reserve a meeting space for the exercise planning team and the actual exercise event.

  - Appoint members of the planning team to arrange materials, supplies, facilities and services in order that the exercise is conducted as planned, without undue disruptions.

- Communication: This is about disseminating exercise information to the internal and external participants.

  - Inform potential participants of the forthcoming exercise.

  - Provide as many details as possible about the progress of the exercise – this helps to instil interest in the exercise and a sense that it is an important corporate event.

  - Notify exercise participants of the exercise date and venue. Preferably attendance should be confirmed three months before the event, accompanied by a reminder every month leading up to the exercise.

  - Provide the exercise concept plan to the participants; this enables them to make the necessary preparations prior to the exercise.

Conduct – Conduct the exercise

The conduct stage is the actual delivery of the exercise. The key activities include:

- Provide an overview of the exercise, including its purpose, objectives and expected duration.
- Provide brief explanations of individual roles and responsibilities during the exercise.
- Explain key actions to be taken in the event of an unforeseen situation.
- Prepare spare copies of the plans.
- During the exercise, provide injects in a timely fashion.
- Prompt questions and record responses from the participants.
- Maintain control throughout the exercise.

Evaluation – Debrief

The purpose of the post-exercise debrief is to encourage participants to share their experience of the exercise. This is an opportunity to identify areas of improvement for existing plans, procedures and team/individual skills. In general, there are two forms of debrief:

- Hot debrief – Immediately after the exercise, the hot debrief is carried out to capture feedback and information about the event whilst the experience is still fresh in the participants' minds. In most cases, this form of debrief is an integral part of discussion-based exercises. This is led by the facilitator to identify outstanding concerns and areas for improvement. This is also an opportunity to ascertain the level of satisfaction with the exercise. Participants should complete their feedback forms after the debrief session.
- Formal debrief – The formal debrief enhances the value of the entire exercise process. It usually takes place a few weeks after the exercise (mainly for operation-based exercises). This form of debrief highlights the management issues that emerged

from the exercise and builds upon the information collated from the hot debrief session. It primarily addresses strengths and weaknesses of organizational response capability at the corporate level as well as identifying opportunities for review and improvement.

Regardless of the type of debrief, the following principles should be followed:

- Emphasize the importance of the debrief session.
- Provide positive comments at the outset of the debrief, such as good practices observed during the exercise; this will encourage an open attitude amongst the participants.
- Make assessments in the form of comparison rather than criticism. It is better to comment that the individual or participants compared favourably to others rather than that they did not perform up to the expectation.
- Engage in open discussion with the participants about their exercise experience, focusing on the following:
  - What went well and what did not go well during the exercise?
  - What could have been done differently to improve the overall BCM response?
  - What improvements should be made to the plans, procedures and staff skills as a result of this exercise?
  - What can be done to improve the participant experience during the exercise?
- Record the debrief discussion and prepare minutes for the exercise participants.

Evaluation – Post-exercise report

The post-exercise report includes a formal exercise evaluation and an integrated analysis that summarizes lessons learned from the event. The information is then developed into a list of recommendations containing proposed actions to enhance the organization's business continuity capability. This is supported by an exercise enhancement programme that summarizes the plan of activities: the actions for improvement, ownership, tasks and required resources, and time-scales for completing the actions.

Summary

The adoption of a range of analytical methodologies in a consistent manner can contribute to an in-depth understanding of what is crucial to fulfilling the organization's obligations. The outcomes of this review provide the basis for developing a fit-for-purpose business continuity capability. This is underpinned by a series of BCM and risk-mitigation strategies to safeguard the continuity of critical functions. However, this requires an appropriate IMS to establish a strategic and operational framework to lead and implement the incident response. To ensure that the BCM strategies are capable of achieving the recovery objectives, there should be exercises to validate plans and procedures as well as the individual/collective capability.

CHECKLIST

This checklist is intended to support the business continuity management system (BCMS) development process	Yes	No	Action required
Has the organization adopted a clearly defined and approved business impact analysis (BIA) process?	☐	☐	☐
Are terms and concepts of the BIA agreed upon and consistently applied?	☐	☐	☐
Is the BIA conducted in an end-to-end product and business service context?	☐	☐	☐
Have the maximum tolerable period of disruption, recovery time objective, recovery point objective and level of business continuity been identified for the critical products and services?	☐	☐	☐
Has the business continuity resource recovery profile been established?	☐	☐	☐
Does the organization have a clearly defined and approved risk assessment (RA) process?	☐	☐	☐
Does the organization ensure that approved risk methodologies, tools and criteria are consistently applied?	☐	☐	☐
Has the organization identified areas of high risk concentration and vulnerability in the delivery system?	☐	☐	☐
Does the organization have a clearly defined and approved BCM strategy option for each critical product and service?	☐	☐	☐
Is the BCM strategy option linked and aligned to support the strategic aims and strategies of the organization?	☐	☐	☐

(Continued)

CHECKLIST *(Continued)*

This checklist is intended to support the business continuity management system (BCMS) development process	Yes	No	Action required
Is the resource recovery strategy consistent with the resource recovery requirement determined by the BIA?	❑	❑	❑
Has the resource recovery strategy been assessed to ensure it is capable of working within the required timescales?	❑	❑	❑
Does the organization have an appropriate incident management structure (IMS) with clear roles, responsibilities and escalating process?	❑	❑	❑
Does the organization have a clearly defined and approved plan development process?	❑	❑	❑
Does the business continuity plan (BCP) reflect the currency of information?	❑	❑	❑
Is there integration of different types of plan in the IMS and with the BCPs of key suppliers?	❑	❑	❑
Does the BCP contain all the pertinent information required for use in an incident?	❑	❑	❑
Does the exercise programme provide for various types and methods of assessing the organization's business continuity capability?	❑	❑	❑
Are exercise roles, responsibilities and authorities clearly defined and documented in the exercise programme?	❑	❑	❑

Further reading

Business Continuity Institute (2013) *Good Practice Guidelines: A guide to global good practice in business continuity*, Business Continuity Institute, Caversham

Bird, L (2011) *Dictionary of Business Continuity Management Terms*, Business Continuity Institute, Caversham

Disaster Recovery Institute International (DRII) (2012) *Professional Practices for Business Continuity Practitioners*, DRII, New York

Disaster Recovery Institute International (2013) *International Glossary for Resiliency*, DRII, New York

IEC 31010:2009 – Risk management – Risk assessment techniques

ISO 31000:2009 – Risk management – Principles and guidelines

ISO 22300:2012 – Societal security – Terminology

ISO 22301:2012 – Societal security – Business continuity management systems – Requirements

ISO 22313:2012 – Societal security – Business continuity management systems – Guidance

ISO 22320:2011 – Societal security – Emergency management – Requirements for incident response

ISO 22398:2013 – Societal security – Guidelines for exercises

ISO Guide 73:2009 – Risk management – Vocabulary

ISO/IEC 24762:2008 – Information technology – Security techniques – Guidelines for information and communications technology disaster recovery services

ISO/IEC 27001:2013 – Information technology – Security techniques – Information security management systems – Requirements

ISO/IEC 27002:2013 – Information technology – Security techniques – Code of practice for information security controls

ISO/IEC 27031:2011 – Information technology – Security techniques – Guidelines for information and communication technology readiness for business continuity

ISO/IEC 27036:2014 – Information technology – Security techniques – Information security for supplier relationships – Part 1: Overview and concepts

Performance evaluation

08

OVERVIEW

- This chapter first highlights the essential attributes of the BCMS performance assessment and why it is important.
- It goes on to describe the performance evaluation criteria and the three common approaches of assessing the effectiveness of the BCMS.
- It then discusses the fundamental principles of a BCMS audit.
- Finally, the chapter outlines the essence and process of undertaking a BCMS management review.

Background

Perhaps as the result of recognizing the value BCMS adds in optimizing product and service availability, an organization might want to know how effective its BCMS is in the current context or whether the management system has achieved its intended outcome. In order to understand the state of the BCMS performance, some form of assessment tools needs to be established.

The rationale of evaluating the performance of the BCMS is to measure its current state against a defined set of requirements. One identifies the inherent gaps in key processes that can affect the integrity of the BCMS. Such information forms the basis for seeking continual improvement. However, before any actions for remediation or improvement can take place, there should be management review to evaluate the performance results. Such a review process reinforces executive participation and ensures that the BCMS remains compatible with the organization's long-term goals.

BCMS performance assessment

Performance evaluation is an essential element of the BCMS. It supports the process of continual improvement of the organization's business continuity capability. Its primary purpose is to establish a monitoring and management programme to ensure the BCMS remains effective. In this context, one assesses the performance of the underlying processes that make up the BCMS. It is important that these processes are properly understood and measured before being compared with the defined requirements or key performance indicators. To put it succinctly, a process cannot be improved unless it can be evaluated.

BCMS evaluation criteria

There are a number of corporate factors that can influence the effectiveness of the BCMS and its ability to achieve the intended outcomes. These factors need to be identified, understood and defined as criteria for the organization to assess against its BCMS performance. The following are some key factors that can be used for the formulation of BCM criteria.

- Business continuity leadership
- Contribution to critical operations
- Design of the BCMS
- BCM teams and individuals
- Adaptability of the BCMS

Business continuity leadership

Business continuity leadership entails the evaluation of the role the senior leadership team plays in the organization's BCMS. Their support for the management system can be judged by the extent the BCMS is incorporated into board-level activities. This includes aligning the BCMS to corporate strategies, appointing a business continuity champion, allocating a dedicated budget for the BCMS and participating in management reviews.

Contribution to critical operations

An attempt to evaluate its effectiveness can involve a review of the critical functions that fall within the scope of the BCMS. This can be gauged by taking into consideration the tangible and intangible benefits the BCMS brings, such as reducing downtime, minimizing wastages, and optimizing resilience in critical workflows.

Design of the BCMS

One of the most significant factors that influences the BCMS performance is the design and integration of the management system in the organizational structure. In particular, the evaluation emphasizes chief management issues like the harmonization between the purpose of the BCMS and organizational goals and strategies, embedment of BCMS in mainstream management and adaptability of the BCMS.

BCM teams and individuals

Organizations must also consider the 'soft' issues of the BCMS. The evaluation tends to focus on the assignment of BCM roles and responsibilities to appropriate individuals, the establishment of competence, individual and team capability and the collective commitment to achieving the BCMS requirements. Predominantly, this factor contributes to the effective performance of the BCMS.

Adaptability of the BCMS

Adaptability refers to the responsiveness of the BCMS to new challenges and opportunities. This, however, is influenced by the maintenance programme, which ensures the ongoing suitability of the BCMS in the corporate setting. In most cases, the evaluation focuses on the review and change processes that improve the business continuity capability. The evaluation also determines whether the maintenance programme is proportionate to the nature of the BCMS, whilst taking into account its operating environment.

Approaches to performance evaluation

The monitoring and assessment of the BCMS is a fundamental process of performance evaluation. It should be carried out in an objective manner and in accordance with the requirements set out in the business continuity policy. In most cases, the corporate decision to evaluate performance will be spurred by one or more of the following motivations:

- Enable the identification of the organization's key BCMS performance drivers
- Develop a consistent approach to assess the BCMS performance
- Provide a consistent good practice benchmark for the BCMS
- Identify performance gaps in the BCMS
- Develop appropriate and incremental actions to improve the current BCMS performance

This book suggests three commonly adopted approaches in the evaluation of the BCMS performance:

- Benchmarking
- Gap analysis
- Audit

Benchmarking

Benchmarking is a systematic and continuous process that enables organizations to measure their performance against their counterparts'. Benchmarking is considered one of the essential business performance management tools that enables forward-looking organizations to improve corporate efforts. The process consists of two premises: First, it helps the organization to sustain management and operational effectiveness by analyzing performance excellence based on the evidence gathered from its environment. Second, it ensures that the organization is continually striving to improve its performance through comparison with organizations of similar characteristics whilst also incorporating the latest BCM practices into its BCMS.

The key benefits of benchmarking for BCMS include the following:

- Determining the drivers that sustain the superior performance of the BCMS
- Identifying best practices in the BCMS
- Defining the performance gap between the organization's BCMS and that of the best practice organization
- Establishing the foundation for continual improvement

This book proposes a two-phase approach comprising six steps to benchmarking the BCMS performance (see Figure 8.1).

FIGURE 8.1 BCMS benchmarking process

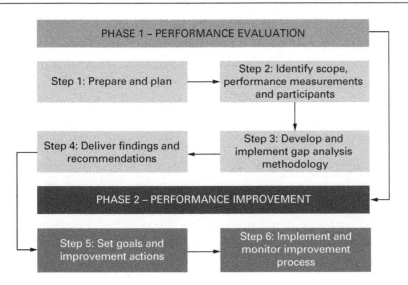

Phase 1 – Performance evaluation is the information analysis stage that gathers and analyzes pertinent information about the relative performance of all involved in the benchmark study. It identifies the gaps between the subject organization's BCMS and that of the participating organizations. It comprises four steps:

- Step 1: Prepare and plan
- Step 2: Identify scope, performance measurements and participants
- Step 3: Develop and implement gap analysis methodology
- Step 4: Deliver findings and recommendations

Phase 2 – Performance improvement establishes an understanding of the drivers that enable superior performance and incorporates them into the continual improvement programme. Phase 2 consists of two additional steps:

- Step 5: Set goals and improvement actions
- Step 6: Implement and monitor improvement process

Step 1: Prepare and plan

- Identify the project objectives. Determine the purpose of the benchmark study (the outcomes it seeks to achieve).
- Determine the key project activities. A project management approach can be adopted when undertaking the benchmark study. This helps to ensure that roles and responsibilities are appropriately assigned and individual tasks are carried out as planned.

Step 2: Identify scope, performance measurements and participants

- Define the scope and the performance measures. The objectives of the benchmark study should be capable of determining the scope of evaluation. This helps to keep the entire project focused and manageable. Though benchmarking can be used to evaluate a particular phase or process of the BCMS, an assessment of its whole lifecycle is imperative for developing a holistic view of the state of the management system. The key performance indicators that will form the basis for the development of a performance scoring system are determined at this stage. It is important that the scoring system is clear and unambiguous to ensure comparability of the information collected.

- Identify the participating organizations in the benchmark study. In particular, if this is an external assessment, creating a list of criteria is useful to identify the relevant participating organizations. Comparable or similar characteristics in terms of size, nature and business type should be the prime considerations. This ensures that the comparison can be carried out and analyzed in meaningful ways.

Step 3: Develop and implement gap analysis methodology

- Determine the methodology. The approach to information collection and analysis should be evaluated to ensure that it meets the requirements of the benchmark study.

- Develop the information collection methods. Design and test the tools for information collection, such as questionnaires or interview questions.

- Analyze the Information. Once the information has been collated but before analysis can take place, validation and normalization are performed. The former establishes the completeness of the information whilst the latter adjusts information to enable like comparisons to be made. The information is then entered into the scoring system. The scores should be able to quantify the performance of the organization's BCMS as well as that of the participating organizations.

Step 4: Deliver findings and recommendations

Draft the benchmark report. Based on the comparative study, the findings and recommendations are prepared in a report for executive management. The report should be clear, concise and easily understood to enable the management team to make decisions on improving the BCMS performance.

Step 5: Set goals and improvement actions

Develop the improvement action plan. The BCM team is usually tasked with proposing actions of improvement for the BCMS. It entails the formulation of goals and actions to achieve the recommendations in the benchmark report. A set of criteria should also be established and incorporated in the action plan for monitoring and assessing the BCMS performance. It is important that the plan is agreed upon and approved by the business continuity director or executive management before the proposed actions are implemented.

Step 6: Implement and monitor improvement process

- Review and improve the existing processes and procedures. It is important that the improvement actions – new processes, procedures and modifications – are implemented via the organization's change management process. These actions should be communicated to staff who hold BCM roles across the organization. Prior to implementation, the BCM team should determine whether additional training is necessary for those who are involved in supporting the performance improvement process.

- Monitor progress. The improvement actions will take time to implement and embed in the BCMS. It is important that they are rolled out appropriately and sustained over time. These actions could be supported by regular review meetings or corrective actions (if necessary). Where further changes are required, they should be documented and communicated to all parties who support the performance improvement process.

Table 8.1 provides an example of a scoring table of a benchmark study. It summarizes how an organization performs in relation to the best practice organization. In this example, four areas of measurement are developed to assess the BCMS: culture, people, leadership and processes. It is important that the four areas of assessment are

TABLE 8.1 Benchmarking scoring table

Elements	Description	Scores					Total Percentage (a)		Average Total (a/5)	
		Level 1 None 0%	Level 2 Basic 25%	Level 3 Intermediate 50%	Level 4 Advanced 75%	Level 5 Mature 100%	BMKO	BPO	BMKO	BPO
A	**Culture**									
1	Have the BCMS and its policy been communicated throughout the organization?				✦	□	75%	100%		
2	Roles and responsibilities	Have staff been made aware of their roles and responsibilities in contributing to the effectiveness of the BCMS?			✦	□	75%	75%		
3	Staff support	Do staff across the organization proactively demonstrate their support and commitment to the business continuity policy and vision?		✦	□		50%	75%		
4	Integration	Does the organization promote a working culture that ensures business continuity is an integral part of corporate activities?		✦	□		50%	75%		
5	Awareness programme	Is there a formal business continuity awareness and training programme for new and existing managers and staff?		✦			□	100%	100%		
							350%	425%	70%	85%
							BMKO	BPO	BMKO	BPO
B	**People**									
6	Qualifications	Are professionally qualified staff involved in the management of the organization's BCMS?			✦	□	75%	100%		
7	Training	Is there an ongoing training and support programme for those directly involved in the management and maintenance of the organization's BCMS?		✦	□		50%	75%		
8	Trends and development	Do staff regularly update themselves with the latest developments in the business continuity industry?			✦	□	75%	75%		
9	Staff performance	Does the organization have clearly defined and documented key performance indicators (KPIs) for staff responsible for the BCMS?		✦	□		50%	75%		
10	Selection criteria	Is there a set of criteria for appointing staff of critical functions to manage their BCM arrangements?			✦	□	75%	75%		
							325%	400%	65%	80%

(Continued)

TABLE 8.1 (Continued)

		Scores					Total Percentage (a)		Average Total (a/5)	
Elements	**Description**	Level 1 None 0%	Level 2 Basic 25%	Level 3 Intermediate 50%	Level 4 Advanced 75%	Level 5 Mature 100%	BMKO	BPO	BMKO	BPO
C	**Leadership**									
11	Strategic alignment	Do executive management ensure that the business continuity policy and objectives are established for the BCMS to align with the strategic direction of the organization?				✷ ☐		75%	75%		
12	Business continuity champion	Is a senior member, the business continuity champion, appointed to oversee the development and management of the organization's BCMS?				✷	✤ ☐	100%	100%		
13	Budget	Does the organization have an annual budget for the management of the BCMS?				✷	✤ ☐	100%	100%		
14	Communication and conformance	Do members of executive management communicate the importance of business continuity and conforming to the BCMS requirements?				✷ ✤	☐	75%	100%		
15	Roles and responsibilities	Is the role of executive management clearly defined, agreed and established in the incident management structure?				✷ ✤ ☐		75%	75%		
								425%	450%	85%	90%
D	**Processes**							BMKO	BPO	BMKO	BPO
16	Standard practice	Do the BCMS and its processes align with good practices and standards?			✷	✤	☐	75%	100%		
17	Policy	Does the organization have a clearly defined, documented and approved business continuity policy?			✷	✤ ☐		75%	75%		
18	Corporate governance	Does the organization's business continuity policy enable corporate governance, and take into account the requirements of its key stakeholders and legal and regulatory obligations?			✷ ✤	☐		50%	75%		
19	Third-party BCM	Are third-party business continuity arrangements incorporated in the organization's BCMS?			✷	✤ ☐		75%	75%		
20	Continual improvement	Does the element of continual improvement form part of the BCMS?			✷		✤ ☐	100%	100%		
								375%	425%	75%	85%

given the same level of emphasis since each can substantially influence the management performance of the BCMS. A number of factors, in the form of questions, are developed for each area (a sample of five questions is provided). The questions form the basis for a discussion with the participating organizations. In order to quantify the overall BCMS performance, a percentage scoring system based on five levels of performance is incorporated. In addition, a baseline can be set for each category to assess whether the factors in their current state have achieved the minimum level of requirements. This helps to draw attention to particular factors that weigh down the overall score.

A simple radar chart presents the scores from Table 8.1 in Figure 8.2. This reveals at a glance how the organization performs against the best practice organization. Likewise, it can determine whether the

FIGURE 8.2 Diagrammatic presentation of BCMS performance

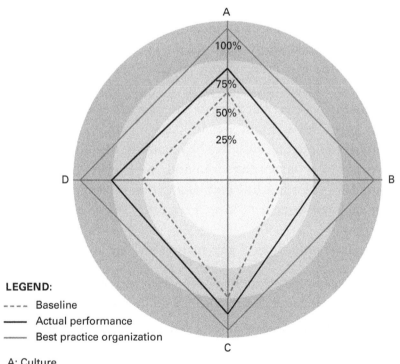

LEGEND:
- - - - Baseline
———— Actual performance
———— Best practice organization

A: Culture
B: People
C: Leadership
D: Processes

organization's current BCM initiative is measuring up to the pursuit of best practice.

It is important to note that though this benchmark scoring template offers a number of perspectives for understanding the BCMS performance, it should not be treated as an oversimplified assessment since organizations have different requirements of evaluating performance. In particular, the areas to be measured are very much dependent on the purpose of the performance evaluation, that is, whether the benchmark study is assessing specific aspects of the BCMS or the entire management system. In addition, the varied levels of BCM maturity amongst participating organizations and how the findings inform the actions of improvement can influence the nature the study.

Gap analysis

At times, organizations may struggle to understand what actions are needed to improve the performance of the business continuity capability. All too often, the improvement efforts either lack focus or are too diverse. Gap analysis is an approach that helps to bring incremental improvements to the BCMS. It involves an investigation of the gap between the actual level of performance and the stipulated requirements, such as vision, goals and objectives. It develops the necessary actions to enhance the effectiveness of the current processes and practices in line with what is required. It is important to note that effective gap analysis, like any other useful tool, needs to be institutionalized aptly to achieve its full benefits. It should form an integral part of the organization's overall performance improvement process. Figure 8.3 shows the BCMS gap analysis cycle.

The primary functions of gap analysis seek to do the following:

- Develop an understanding of the difference between the current performance and the defined requirements
- Establish an assessment of the barriers that need to be addressed
- Develop an action plan to close the gap between the current status and the defined requirements

FIGURE 8.3 BCMS gap analysis model

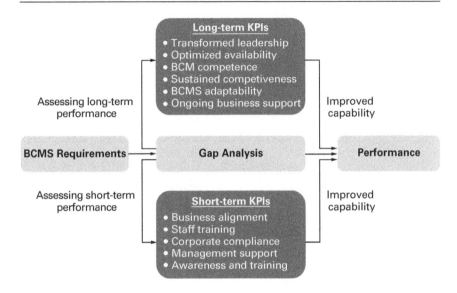

At the outset, gap analysis must adopt realistic performance meas-urements if its primary functions are to be achieved. It can effectively assess how different aspects of the BCMS currently perform in rela-tion to the desired level of performance. The process determines the deficiencies in the BCMS in order to develop improvement actions to address those issues.

Gap analysis works best when it is used as a staged process. It helps to bring improvements more readily in specific areas of the BCMS than does benchmarking, which tends to assess the over-all performance of the management system. As such, gap analysis requires the improvement efforts to be focused on the most critical aspects that could influence the integrity of the BCMS. Nonetheless, once the gap and barriers have been addressed, attention can divert to other areas in the management system. Adopting this progressive approach ensures a gradual implementation of improvement to the entire BCMS.

Gap analysis should be not a complex process. It can be easily controlled and tailored to meet the requirements of the performance evaluation study. Table 8.2 outlines the basic steps and methods of performing a gap analysis.

TABLE 8.2 Basic steps and methods of performing a gap analysis

Phase	Development Stage	Techniques
Preparation	• Identify current BCM standards and policies	• Reference to relevant corporate policies, plans and requirements • Research and reference to relevant legal, regulatory and statutory guidance • Identify relevant standards and good practice guidelines developed by national and international standards development bodies and professional bodies
	• Define scope of gap analysis	• Reference to business continuity policy • Review BCM reports • Seek advice and agreement from business continuity champion
	• Gain executive approval	• Present and confirm scope with executive management • Seek approval for project, including resources and timescales
	• Develop gap analysis methodology	• Identify sources of information • Identify respondent criteria • Decide and create information collection methods • Pilot test information collection methods
Implementation	• Collect Information	• Perform information gathering using questionnaires, interviews and/or documentary review • Interview business owners and other key staff • Gather all relevant BCM materials, such as plans and reports
	• Evaluate current BCM processes	• Substantiate findings against documentary evidence • Identify discrepancies and conduct follow-up actions • Seek validation from business owners • Prepare gap analysis report
Post-review	• Document findings and recommendations	• Present findings and recommendations to business continuity champion and executive management
	• Develop action plan	• Use findings and recommendations to develop improvement actions • Develop a schedule of implementation

TABLE 8.3 Gap analysis scoring checklist

		Scores						Barriers to Achieving the Requirements
Requirements	None	Level 1	Level 2	Level 3	Level 4	Level 5		
	0	20	40	60	80	100		
Business Impact Analysis (BIA)								
1 The current BIA is conducted in an end-to-end business service and product context.				●				
2 The critical functions and processes, including outsourced services, are clearly identified, defined and documented.				●				
3 The recovery time objectives (RTOs), recovery point objectives (RPOs) and levels of business continuity (LBC) for the critical functions and processes are clearly defined and documented.			●					
4 The BIA has identified the resource recovery requirements of each critical function.				●				
5 The BIA is carried out as a part of the organization's key management activities, such as the development of new products and services, and functional and procedural improvements.			●					

(Continued)

TABLE 8.3 (Continued)

Requirements	Scores						Barriers to Achieving the Requirements
	None	Level 1	Level 2	Level 3	Level 4	Level 5	
	0	20	40	60	80	100	
Risk Assessment (RA)							
6 There is a clearly defined and documented process to ensure that the approved risk methodology, tools, techniques and criteria are consistently applied.					●		
7 The corporate risk appetite, including the acceptance of residual risks, is clearly defined, documented and approved.				●			
8 A risk assessment has been completed within the last 12 months in respect of the organization's critical functions and processes.			●				
9 The organizational and industry-systemic risks are clearly identified, assessed and documented.			●				
10 Areas of high risk concentration within critical functions are identified, assessed and managed.					●		

Level 1: Little evidence – requires holistic review of processes and procedures to derive evidence

Level 2: Some evidence – lack of documentation

Level 3: Some evidence – documented

Level 4: Good evidence – majority of processes and procedures are documented and in place

Level 5: Full evidence – complies with the stipulated requirements

Table 8.3 provides a sample checklist of requirements for undertaking a gap analysis of the business impact analysis and risk assessment. A rating scale from 0 to 100 points, with their respective levels, is used to gauge the performance of current processes and practices against the defined requirements. In this context, the stipulated requirement is set at 80 points. To determine which factors impede performance, an additional column – barriers to achieving the requirements – can be provided to capture feedback from respondents.

Based on the findings, a simple gap analysis graph (Figure 8.4) can be generated to illustrate the gap between the current performance and the required standard.

Audit

An audit involves a review of the management processes and documentation of the BCMS against operating guidance from the

FIGURE 8.4 Gap analysis graph

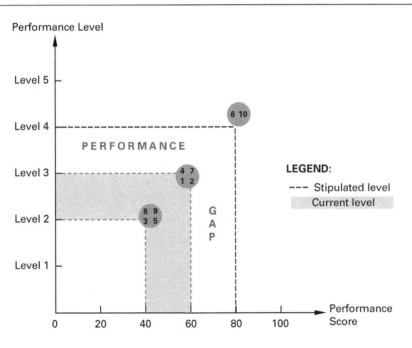

business continuity policy. Depending on the application, an audit can also be called self-assessment. An audit is primarily concerned with the identification of inconsistencies in the processes that inhibit the BCMS from achieving its intended outcomes. It should be performed at planned intervals to provide information for management review and support the setting of objectives for continual improvement.

An audit fulfils five main functions:

- Verifies the BCMS conformity to the organization's business continuity policy framework

- Validates the BCMS against current good practices or standards adopted by the organization

- Verifies the extent to which the BCMS is embedded in critical processes

- Highlights deficiencies in the BCMS in order that actions are developed to remedy nonconformities

- Reviews the skills and capabilities of staff responsible for managing the BCMS

Broadly, there are three forms of BCMS audit and each serves a different purpose:

- Internal audit – Conducted internally for management review or other internal purposes, such as understanding the current state of the BCMS and demonstrating internal compliance with defined standards and guidelines.

- Supplier audit – Also known as the second-party audit because it engages an independent external party, or parties, such as customers or their representatives who have an interest in the organization. These parties scrutinize the BCMS in order to verify it against predefined requirements. In some cases, supplier audit is a preparatory assessment prior to a third-party audit.

- Third-party audit – Carried out for regulatory purposes or certification to a management system standard. It can involve a regulatory assessor or an independent external party, also known as the certification body, to assess the organization's BCMS. It attests to conformity of processes and procedures based on the requirements of a particular regulatory guidance or standard.

Fundamental principles of an audit

When undertaking an audit, there are a number of principles that should be observed to ensure the tasks are adequately carried out. Adhering to these principles also provides reliable and conclusive information on which the organization can act to improve its BCMS performance:

- Independence – The audit process should be performed in an impartial manner so that the results will be unbiased. As such, it is important that staff who undertake the audit role, that is, the auditors, need to be independent from the functions being audited and free from conflict of interest. In addition, they should remain objective throughout the process to ensure the findings are reported truthfully and accurately.

- Prudence – Due diligence and judgement should be applied in the course of obtaining audit evidence. This includes due care in the use and protection of information acquired and preservation of the confidentiality of audit results.

- Repetition – For an audit to be reliable, the audit methods, including the procedures, should be repetitive and capable of deriving similar results without deviating from the defined audit objectives. This is particularly important when dealing with a process-based audit undertaken by a team of auditors. Explanatory notes should be provided to *all* team members. This helps to develop a common understanding of the methods and procedures so that the process is carried out consistently.

- Evidence-driven – To ensure the findings are accurate and conclusive, the audit should be based on evidence in the form of documentary materials – ones that are capable of substantiating the auditees' responses and findings. Because of the finite duration of the audit project, it may be necessary to adopt a sampling method to select representative evidence from myriad materials. It is important to note that when using materials produced by the functions, verification is necessary to ensure that the content is sufficiently reliable for the audit purpose. As such, consideration should be given to the accuracy, appropriateness and completeness of the evidence.

Scope of BCMS audit

The organization's business continuity policy concerning the audit or self-assessment should clearly set out what it intends to achieve. It is most likely that the themes of the audit will comprise one or more of the following:

- Management oversight – To evaluate if a clearly defined BCMS framework is established to provide the governance and management of BCM activities. It is also important to determine whether there is executive commitment to review and maintain the business continuity policy, framework and processes at planned intervals

- Skills and capability – To appraise the managerial and operational roles, responsibilities and competencies of staff responsible for managing the BCMS. In addition, there should be assessment on the adequacy of staff training and development programmes that enhance management skills and capabilities

- Processes – To evaluate whether BCM activities are managed in an approved manner to fulfil the intended outcomes in the business continuity policy

- Integration and embedment – To determine the extent to which the BCMS is integrated into the organization's mainstream activities and whether its requirements are compatible with the corporate long-term direction and strategies

Components of BCMS audit

The BCMS audit process is made up of a number of components that ensure the review is undertaken in an effective and efficient manner. The components are interrelated and have their own set of activities. Figure 8.5 shows the key components and elements (in italics) of the BCMS audit programme and process.

Table 8.4 provides an explanation of the key elements in the audit components.

FIGURE 8.5 BCMS audit programme and process

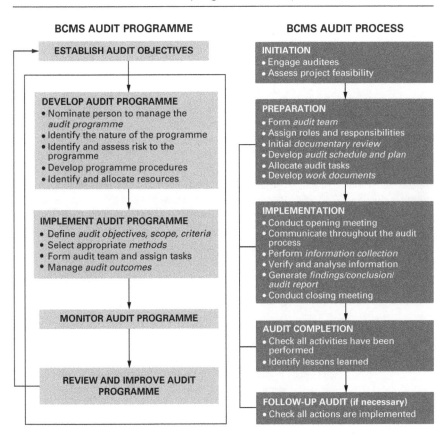

BCMS AUDIT PROGRAMME

ESTABLISH AUDIT OBJECTIVES

DEVELOP AUDIT PROGRAMME
- Nominate person to manage the *audit programme*
- Identify the nature of the programme
- Identify and assess risk to the programme
- Develop programme procedures
- Identify and allocate resources

IMPLEMENT AUDIT PROGRAMME
- Define *audit objectives, scope, criteria*
- Select appropriate *methods*
- Form audit team and assign tasks
- Manage *audit outcomes*

MONITOR AUDIT PROGRAMME

REVIEW AND IMPROVE AUDIT PROGRAMME

BCMS AUDIT PROCESS

INITIATION
- Engage auditees
- Assess project feasibility

PREPARATION
- Form *audit team*
- Assign roles and responsibilities
- Initial *documentary review*
- Develop *audit schedule and plan*
- Allocate audit tasks
- Develop *work documents*

IMPLEMENTATION
- Conduct opening meeting
- Communicate throughout the audit process
- Perform *information collection*
- Verify and analyse information
- Generate *findings/conclusion/ audit report*
- Conduct closing meeting

AUDIT COMPLETION
- Check all activities have been performed
- Identify lessons learned

FOLLOW-UP AUDIT (if necessary)
- Check all actions are implemented

TABLE 8.4 Audit elements and their explanation

Items	Description
Audit objectives	The objectives set out what needs to be achieved by the audit. This is often related to the requirements of the business continuity policy. Objectives include determining the conformity of the BCMS and its processes to specified standards, evaluating the achievement of the business continuity objectives and identifying areas of improvement to the BCMS.
Audit scope	This defines the boundary of the audit. The scope is often dictated by the relationship between locations, functions and processes that deliver the organization's critical products and services.
Audit schedule	This is an output of the audit programme that provides details about the audit and how the audit process is facilitated.
Audit programme	The audit programme regulates the audit activities. It is a 'master plan' that consists of the main activities, including resources and timescales necessary to deliver the audit tasks and objectives. The extent of the BCMS audit programme should be appropriate to the size and complexity of the audit project. At the minimum, the audit programme should contain the scope, objectives, frequencies, audit schedules, criteria, resources, and methods and processes.
Audit criteria	Broadly, the audit criteria comprise the business continuity policy, BCM standards, industry regulations and current good practice guidelines.
Methods	This refers to how the audit is conducted. A combination of methods can be used, such as interviews, documents reviews, observations and site visits. However, the choice of methods is largely dependent on the nature of the audit, that is, onsite or a remote location. It is always useful to adopt the triangulation approach to information collection; this ensures that the information can be verified by another chosen method.
Audit team	The composition of the audit team is influenced by the extent and complexity of the audit. When selecting the audit team members, consideration should be given to the required knowledge and experience in auditing and the subject of business continuity; this ensures that the team can undertake the audit tasks competently and fulfil the audit objectives. The audit activities should also be properly tasked and managed in order to avoid placing unnecessary burden on particular individuals.

(Continued)

TABLE 8.4 (*Continued*)

Items	Description
Audit outcomes	This commonly includes the audit findings, recommendations and remedial actions agreed upon and approved by management.
Audit plan	This covers the activities to be performed by the auditor. The audit plan can act as a checklist to ensure the tasks are carried out as planned. The plan includes the audit objectives, scope and criteria, roles and responsibilities, reference documents, resource issues, audit ethics, and follow-up actions/activities.
Work documents	These materials are used to support the audit activities. They comprise checklists, aide-memoirs, a sampling plan and forms for recording key information in the audit.
Documentary review	This is an information collection method that is used to collate all relevant information about the organization's BCMS. In most cases, the main documents used for the review include the business continuity policy, BCPs and reports recording the BCM activities, such as the business impact analysis, risk assessment, strategies development, exercise and maintenance, and continual improvement.
Information collection	The selected methods are implemented to collate the relevant information. They include face-to-face interviews, questionnaires, site visits and observations.
Audit findings	The findings are assessed against the audit criteria and should be based on evidence. This determines whether the BCMS and its processes are in line with the requirements. This is an opportunity to determine the areas of focus – nonconformities and where further improvements are required. In addition, good practices in the BCMS should be identified and shared across the organization and its functions.
Audit conclusion	The audit findings are related back to the objectives to determine if they have been achieved before the audit conclusion is reached. The audit conclusion will then comment on the outcome of the audit, that is, the state of the organization's BCMS, and propose actions of improvement.
Audit report	The report highlights the key audit findings – conformities and nonconformities, good practices, areas of concern and proposed recommendations to improve the BCMS.

Management review

The central tenet of management review is the executive support for the continual improvement of the BCMS. It is a strategic, forward-looking review process that evaluates whether the BCMS is producing the desired results to achieve its intended outcomes. It goes beyond the usual planning and review meeting: it focuses on the 'what-ifs' and plans for improvement. This entails the identification of inadequacies in management procedures and determination of appropriate actions to improve effectiveness. As such, it is important that management review is conducted at planned intervals in addition to when there are significant changes to the BCMS and its processes.

To ensure the management review addresses the overall performance of the BCMS, executive management should consider what the meeting intends to achieve, which could include one or more of the following objectives:

- Assess the factors, including risks issues that may jeopardize the BCMS performance

- Evaluate the BCMS performance against the review objectives

- Review the progression of the BCMS with past reviews

- Resolve anomalies in the BCMS

- Review and confirm budgetary support for the BCMS

- Confirm the courses of actions and recommendations to enhance the current BCMS performance

- Address any management issues that inhibit the effective implementation of the BCMS

Membership of management review

The group that carries out the management review should be represented by key members from the BCM working group (see Chapter 4: Figure 4.2). This strategic group, known as the management review committee, assumes oversight of the proper functioning of the BCMS. This includes making decisions on its long-term direction and integrating its requirements into critical operations.

For any management review to be undertaken successfully, it should be representative and authoritative, with the ability to reach conclusive decisions. At the minimum, it should comprise the following roles, though certain individuals may assume more than one role in the review process:

- Senior leadership team – This group of staff is usually made up of the business continuity director and board-level directors of major functions in the organizations. They are considered the decision-makers of the management review. Their involvement emphasizes the drive for success in the BCMS.

- Technical review lead – The technical lead is often the group business continuity manager, who is responsible for coordinating the management review and ensuring that the process is appropriately carried out to meet its intended purpose. In addition, the technical review lead provides the necessary subject matter advice to executive management to fulfil its responsibilities.

- Management review administrator – The administrator records actions, decisions, anomalies and recommendations made by the review committee.

Components of management review

The management review of the BCMS is conducted based on three underlying components: inputs, considerations and outputs. It critically evaluates the BCMS against defined requirements through a review of programme documentation and implementation records. The conclusion of the review is generally an agreed upon set of recommendations and actions for addressing existing and potential performance gaps or nonconformities.

- Inputs – The inputs generally comprise a compilation of all relevant facts about the current state of the organization's BCMS, its management approach, independent audit or self-assessment, and other pertinent information about corporate preparedness.

- Considerations – Once the key information about the BCMS has been assembled, a structured approach to reviewing the information should be adopted. It should highlight precisely how well the BCMS and its processes match up to the defined requirements. The evaluation of information should be open and without bias and should allow feedback and innovative proposals.

- Outputs – The outputs usually consist of a set of decisions made, along with actions that enable the BCMS to continue to support corporate needs. It is important that key individuals are assigned with clear timescales for implementing the agreed upon actions.

Figure 8.6 outlines the underlying components in the management review process.

It is a good management practice to create and maintain documentation for the management review. This provides the organization a trail of management decisions for improving the BCMS performance, whilst demonstrating that the review process is adequately carried out.

Summary

Understanding how the organization's BCMS is performing is vital because without such knowledge it is difficult to assess the relevance of BCM activities in the current environment. There are many tools at the disposal of organizations to pursue performance improvement in the BCMS. Each has its strengths and weaknesses, and selection will largely depend on the requirements of the evaluation. Management review is an integral process of performance evaluation and is therefore essential for assessing the suitability of the BCMS in supporting the organization's goals and strategies. One that requires management leadership in ensuring that key decisions are taken to optimize its currency and effectiveness.

FIGURE 8.6 Components of management review

INPUTS

- A statement of objectives for the management review
- BCMS audit findings
- Information on critical suppliers' business continuity preparedness
- Performance evaluation results
- Status of preventive and corrective actions
- Risk reports and registers
- Follow-up actions from previous management reviews
- Corporate long-range planning report
- Decisions and actions for performance improvement
- BCM standards and guidance
- Incidents reports
- Exercise reports
- Feedback on the awareness training programme
- Resources forecast
- Outstanding issues

CONSIDERATIONS

- Is the business continuity policy still relevant to the current context?
- Are roles and responsibilities clearly defined and do they make sense?
- Are the resources appropriately allocated and assigned?
- Is the BCMS meeting the organization's regulatory obligations?
- Are the procedures clear and adequate? Consider addition, modification or elimination.
- What are the barriers to the current BCMS performance?
- How effective are the current assessment procedures?
- Can new measurable performance objectives be established?
- Are there changes to the regulations? Are there requirements to change the management approach to the BCMS?
- What are the new stakeholder and regulatory requirements since the last review?
- Are there potential methods to improve the BCMS and its processes?

OUTPUTS

- Management review objectives reviewed
- Modification to the scope of the BCMS
- Confirmed actions to improve the effectiveness of the BCMS
- Changes to the processes and procedures in response to new and emerging organizational and environmental drivers
- Action items list with ownership and target dates of implementation
- Approved resource needs
- Approved budget for the BCMS

CHECKLIST

This checklist is intended to support the business continuity management system (BCMS) development process	Yes	No	Action required
Does the organization have a clearly defined and approved BCMS performance assessment process and frequency?	☐	☐	☐
Does the organization have a set of clearly defined and approved key performance indicators for the BCMS?	☐	☐	☐
Does the organization have an adequate management review to assess opportunities for improvement and the need for changes to the BCMS?	☐	☐	☐
Does the management review provide clearly defined, prioritized and approved actions to improve the performance of the BCMS?	☐	☐	☐

Further reading

Business Continuity Institute (2013) *Good Practice Guidelines: A guide to global good practice in business continuity*, Business Continuity Institute, Caversham

ISO 19011:2011 – Guidelines for auditing management systems

ISO 22301:2012 – Societal security – Business continuity management systems – Requirements

ISO 22313:2012 – Societal security – Business continuity management systems – Guidance

ISO/IEC 17021:2011 – Conformity assessment – Requirements for bodies providing audit and certification of management systems

Improvement

09

OVERVIEW

- This chapter first introduces the essential attributes of the BCMS control system and discusses the two types of control.
- It goes on to explain the types of nonconformities commonly present in the BCMS.
- Next, it discusses the principal elements, characteristics and process of an effective BCMS control system.
- Finally, the chapter introduces the component of continual improvement in enhancing the effectiveness of the BCMS.

Background

The control system forms a crucial component of the BCMS. Its primary function is to check and take necessary actions to eliminate nonconformities that could prevent the BCMS from achieving its intended outcomes. In order to establish an adequate BCMS control system, a number of principal elements and features should be taken into consideration. In addition, to maintain the effectiveness of the BCMS in its current context, the process of continual improvement should be established as part of the BCMS performance management programme. This process ensures that positive changes are being made to maintain the suitability of the BCMS. Primarily, continual improvement focuses on the key aspects of the BCMS: management, people, processes and procedures, and information, which collectively contribute to the performance of the management system.

BCMS control system

Control forms the motivation to achieve compliance and develop staff BCM capability. It provides checks on people and processes, that is, how adequate the capability or process is to the overall effectiveness of the BCMS. This places emphasis on the comparison of actual results against planned targets.

In the broadest sense, the types of BCMS controls can be grouped into active and passive:

- Active – This includes business continuity leadership and planned checks through a range of BCM activities, such as exercises, self-assessments, audits and performance evaluations.

- Passive – This includes staff communication, policies, procedures and various BCM awareness-raising activities.

The controls form an integral part of the BCMS control system. This vital control system involves the monitoring and control of staff actions and procedures, and enforces compliance with operating requirements.

In essence, the functions of the BCMS control system can serve to do the following:

- Monitor the conformity of inputs (such as actions, processes and procedures) and outputs (such as benefits and outcomes) of the BCMS

- Ensure corrective actions are adequate to support the BCMS requirements

- Direct and support the effectiveness of the BCMS by enforcing process compliance with the requirements of the business continuity policy

- Identify performance discrepancies of those responsible for the day-to-day management of the BCMS

In most cases, lack of an adequate control system is a major feature of poor BCMS performance. This is due to a range of nonconformities present in the BCMS processes.

Types of nonconformities in a BCMS

Broadly, nonconformities in the BCMS can occur in one or more of the following areas:

- Business continuity policy – A nonconformity would be the absence of a business continuity policy, strategies and operational framework to provide guidance on the implementation of the BCMS. In addition, ill-defined business continuity objectives and failure to include key items, such as scope, objectives, requirements, review periods, roles and responsibilities, are common causes of nonconformities.

- Personnel roles and responsibilities – These nonconformities are generally deficiencies in required knowledge, skills and experiences in managing the BCMS. Nonconformities also include the designation of BCM roles and responsibilities to unqualified staff.

- Training – The absence of an ongoing staff development programme to maintain the currency of staff's BCM knowledge and skills would constitute a nonconformity. Another would be the absence of an awareness programme within the organization.

- Processes and procedures – Failure to comply with the operating requirements of the business continuity policy and the absence of key management processes in the BCMS are main forms of nonconformity.

- Executive management – This might constitute an absence of management leadership to provide oversight for the effective implementation of the BCMS.

- Documentation – This generally includes the absence of an adequate documentation system to maintain BCM information and records. This can also include the failure to provide documentary evidence of an effective operation of the BCMS.

Elements of a BCMS control system

The control system plays a vital role in enabling the BCMS to achieve its intended outcomes. In essence, it comprises four principal elements:

1 Objectives and targets

2 Assessment criteria

3 Methods of measurement

4 Rectification

Objectives and targets

In most cases, the business continuity objectives and requirements form the framework against which the control system process operates. It is important that these expectations are communicated to staff in order that they understand the importance of complying with the specifications when undertaking the BCM activities. Wherever possible, the required tasks should be given some form of measurable attributes or targets.

Assessment criteria

The BCM requirements or standards to which the organization aspires can form the basis for the assessment criteria. It is important that the approach to assessment is expressed in quantitative terms in order to obtain an accurate measurement of the BCMS conformity. Those who are involved in the management of the BCMS should be made aware of the performance criteria and the importance of adhering to the requirements.

Methods of assessment

Appropriate methods should be implemented to assess the degree of conformity of the BCMS. In most cases, audit and self-assessment are the key methods adopted to give evidence of conformity with the performance criteria. They highlight how adequate the BCMS is in its current state and verify whether the BCMS requirements have been achieved. In addition, the methods are useful in understanding the root causes of nonconformity.

Rectification

When nonconformities have been identified, corrective actions should be developed to eliminate these inconsistencies in the BCMS. These actions should address the root causes of nonconformities and be capable of guarding against their recurrence. If necessary, prevention actions should be developed to prevent factors that could give rise to potential nonconformities. This is also an opportunity to consider what actions can be taken to improve the BCMS performance.

It is important that the business continuity manager regularly reviews the adequacy of the control system and makes necessary adjustment to its key elements to ensure it remains relevant to support the BCMS.

Characteristics of effective BCMS control system

An effective BCMS control system should be able to provide factual information on the nonconformities and their root causes. It should alert managers to serious management issues and help to facilitate the development of appropriate solutions. An effective BCM control system is strengthened by a number of key features:

1 Information accuracy

2 Comprehensibility

3 Focus

4 Integration

5 Criteria

Information accuracy

Reliable monitoring controls are needed to provide accurate and timely information about the state of the BCMS. Broadly, controls are in the form of planned activities such as exercises, performance evaluations, audits and self-assessments, which can uncover areas of weaknesses or deviations from specified requirements.

Comprehensibility

It is important that the BCMS control system is easily understood by staff involved in managing the BCMS. When the control system is understood properly, it can be implemented consistently, and staff can respond competently to the information they gather. In contrast, a complicated control system can cause misinterpretation and be detrimental to the BCMS.

Focus

Being a regulatory process of the BCMS, the control system should focus on the key factors that can cause nonconformity associated with the implementation and management of the BCMS. By concentrating on the critical aspects of the BCMS, staff can direct their efforts on those issues that are likely to impede effective performance.

Integration

The control system should be appropriate for the nature and complexity of the BCMS. A fit-for-purpose control system has a greater likelihood of embedding in the main processes of the BCMS. Over time, the control system will become an integral part of the management system, and when there is a need to assess the level of conformity of particular processes, it can provide the information required.

Criteria

The performance criteria used by the controls should be developed based on good practice guidelines or requirements set out in the business continuity policy. They should be definite, realistic and measurable. When the criteria are defined in clear terms, the BCMS can be reliably assessed. In contrast, ambiguous or overly ambitious criteria could cause the control system to be counter-productive.

BCMS control system process

The control system is a process of controlling activities and implementing corrective actions, and is made up of five basic steps:

1 Identification
2 Evaluation
3 Action plan
4 Implementation
5 Follow-up

Identification

Identification should be supported by documentary evidence that nonconformities exist in the BCMS. Examples of evidence where nonconformities can be identified include the following:

- The business continuity policy containing objectives and requirements
- Incident reports
- Audit reports
- The BCMS performance enhancement plan
- Training and competency records of BCM staff
- Awareness and training programmes
- Exercise reports
- Performance evaluation reports
- Management review reports

Evaluation

Evaluation primarily determines the root and contributory causes of nonconformities in the BCMS. A list of identified nonconformities should be created based on the evidence gathered during the Identification stage. This will form the basis for gathering relevant information to investigate the probable causes of nonconformities. When determining the causes, it is useful to develop a defined set of activities or a checklist to ensure that nothing is overlooked. This can be a series of instructions that outline what should be performed to determine the causes and whether similar problems are present elsewhere in the BCMS.

Investigating the causes of nonconformities often requires an in-depth examination until the fundamental reason is found. For instance, consider a business continuity coordinator's failure to update a business continuity plan. The investigation revealed that the coordinator had not been properly trained and had forgotten his role in the maintenance process. Based on the initial investigation, the improperly trained coordinator was the immediate cause of the problem but might not be the root cause. Further investigation revealed that the coordinator had recently joined the business function and did not receive proper training. The root cause of the problem was the lack of a structured training programme for staff on the BCM team. Additional information also revealed that there was an absence of documentation to record the training needs of staff in order to maintain their skills.

As part of the evaluation, it is also important to understand the magnitude of the nonconformity, that is, its effects on the BCMS. This information will ensure that the corrective actions required are proportionate to the impact of the nonconformity.

Action plan

For the control system to be effective, the devised actions should address the root causes of nonconformities. These actions are generally reactive and used to address the problems after they are evident. Their purpose is to control and permanently remediate the nonconformities and their impact.

When preparing an action plan, it is useful to list all corrective actions that should be implemented in the BCMS. At the minimum, the list should include key items such as tasks and activities, timescales, resources, and individuals who are responsible for the actions. To ensure that nonconformities do not recur, any changes made to the BCM processes and documentation should be communicated to all individuals who are involved in supporting the BCMS.

Implementation

All corrective actions described in the action plan are initiated to address the nonconformities in the BCMS. Once implemented, they should be checked and documented in the BCMS performance improvement report. The report will facilitate the verification of the actions taken and use for follow-up purpose.

Follow-up

One of the most fundamental steps in the control system is to verify the adequacy of the adopted corrective actions. Questions such as the following can be used to guide the assessment:

- Have the objectives of the corrective actions been achieved?
- Do the actions prevent recurrence of the nonconformities?
- Do the actions underpin the entire control system process?
- Have all nonconformities been completed and verified?
- Is there any possibility that the actions implemented may have adverse effects on the integrity of the BCMS or the control system?
- Have adequate communication and training been implemented to ensure all staff involved in the BCMS understand that the actions have been taken to eliminate the causes of nonconformities?
- Are the actions taken proportionate to the benefits achieved?

A thorough verification should be adopted to ensure that root and contributory causes of the nonconformities have been resolved. There should also be adequate actions to minimize recurrence. Once the follow-up process is complete, the entire process should be reviewed and approved by the business continuity manager.

Documenting the entire control system process, from identifying the nonconformity to the successful implementation of corrective actions, is crucial for managing an effective BCMS. Documentation demonstrates that there are adequate measures in place to maintain the management effectiveness of the BCMS. Perhaps the more important reason is that documentation provides evidence that efforts have been invested to ensure that the BCMS can achieve its intended outcomes.

Continual improvement

Continual improvement is an ongoing effort that makes incremental progress to the effectiveness of the BCMS. It is a forward-looking process that incorporates best practices into the BCMS to ensure that it continues to support the changing requirements of the organization.

In order to assess the adequacy of the BCMS, the business continuity manager needs to address four key questions:

1 Does the BCMS contain the necessary components and processes? The business continuity manager should ensure that the BCMS encapsulates all essential components of an effective management system. One starting point could be the use of good practice guidelines and standards to identify the performance gaps or areas for improvement.

2 How efficient is the BCMS in the current context? It is essential that the BCMS is responsive and addresses the key challenges faced by the organization. Improving the BCMS requires integrated changes in staff, processes and procedures. Such changes ensure that the BCMS remains relevant and is aligned with the strategic direction of the organization.

3 Is the BCMS operating effectively? The business continuity manager should assess how well the BCMS is operating. The manager should know how the BCMS is performing against the stipulated requirements, where the wastages are and whether changes are required to improve the current mode of management. Such answers can be obtained from the evidence of performance evaluation reports and information from the BCMS control system.

4 Is the BCMS providing the business advantages? It is necessary to determine whether the BCMS is generating business advantages to the organization. Such advantages include the minimization of downtime, improved resilience of key activities and generation of competitive advantage through the continuity of operation.

Through continual review of these questions, progressive change can be effectively managed, and continual improvement will become an integral part of the BCMS lifecycle. In addition, it creates steady development in the BCMS by making it an enabler that adds value to the organization's critical processes.

In essence, continual improvement should encapsulate a combination of the key concepts shown in Table 9.1.

Areas of continual improvement

The central tenet of continual improvement is that all aspects of the BCMS can be improved. Broadly, BCMS improvement falls into the following areas:

- Management
- People
- Processes and procedures
- Information

TABLE 9.1 Core concepts of effective continual improvement

Concepts of Effective Continual Improvement
• Secure total commitment from the executive management team
• Set realistic targets for improvement
• Ensure all staff involved in the BCMS understand their roles and contribution to the continual improvement process
• Measure and evaluate progress against key performance indicators and benchmarks
• Adopt recognized good BCM practices and standards
• Establish priorities for improvement
• Promote good communications throughout the organization
• Harness the knowledge and skills of staff in the continual improvement process
• Develop and train staff to manage continual improvement
• Adopt piecemeal approach to continual improvement

Management

Continual improvement is about the ongoing challenge of managing the BCMS. It emphasizes optimizing process efficiency and minimizing nonconformities. Because of the changing nature of the corporate context, ongoing revision to the business continuity policy, requirements, processes and strategies are essential for effective alignment between the BCMS and the organization's business strategies and goals.

People

It is important to enhance BCM knowledge and skills through ongoing training and development. Staff management capability should be subject to a series of progressive exercises in order to identify performance gaps for improvement. In addition, members of the BCM team should keep themselves abreast of the latest developments in the BCM industry, which could also be introduced in the BCMS.

Processes and procedures

To ensure that the BCMS remains effective and able to achieve its intended requirements, its key processes and procedures should undergo planned reviews. Good BCM practices should be incorporated into the incident management structure to facilitate the ongoing adequacy of the command and control system. In addition, there should be adequate monitoring and controls to enforce conformity and foster continual improvement in the BCMS.

Information

Acquiring reliable information is the foundation of establishing an effective BCMS. This includes the adoption of good methodologies for collecting information generated by BCM activities, such as the BIA/RA, audit and performance evaluation. It is important that the procedures for verifying the quality of information are subject to ongoing reviews to ensure that they remain adequate.

Table 9.2 summarizes the various methods and processes for improving the four key areas of the BCMS. These proposed methodologies are not an exhaustive list but rather suggest some useful approaches to fostering continual improvement.

TABLE 9.2 Methods and processes of improvement in BCMS

Core Areas	Methods	Processes
Management	• Management reviews • Business impact and risk assessments • Documentary reviews • Organizational management research • Business process re-engineering	• Set targets based on realistic expectations towards BCMS improvement • Plan staged improvement in the BCMS lifecycle • Establish priorities in key areas that particularly need improvement • Designate a member of executive management as the champion to drive continual improvement • Involve executive management in the continual improvement process • Hold regular meetings with staff to identify key issues and areas that require attention • Establish a BCMS Enhancement Board • Integrate the element of improvement in daily work activities
People	• Focus groups • Awareness programmes • Workshops • Clinics • Training and development programmes	• Communicate the importance of continual improvement in the BCMS • Involve staff in BCMS improvement activities • Ensure all are aware of the tasks of continual improvement and their roles and responsibilities in contributing to its success • Build teams for systematic improvement activities • BCM team to support the business continuity champion's drive for BCMS continual improvement

(Continued)

TABLE 9.2 (Continued)

Core Areas	Methods	Processes
Processes and procedures	• BCMS lifecycle • Business impact and risk assessments • Organizational management theories • Use of quality management cycles • Use of problem-solving tools and good practice techniques • Learning from past experiences and lessons	• Use tools and techniques such as brainstorming, process mapping, flow charts and cause and effect diagrams to review existing BCM processes • Target improvements on areas that are most critical to the integrity of the BCMS • Gather ideas to improve processes and procedures from peer review, training and guidelines, or build from experiences and past lessons • Plan and develop piecemeal improvement projects based on prioritized issues, that is, areas that will impact the BCMS performance
Information	• Organizational analysis • BCMS reports • Information collection methods • Information criteria • Information audits • Performance evaluations	• Assess the information collection process • Evaluate existing framework for verifying quality of information in terms of reliability, accuracy and currency • Review key documents of the BCMS, such as business continuity policy, risk management strategies, plans and reports • Review annual reports on key BCM activities, such as business impact analysis, risk assessment, audit, self-assessment and exercise • Review annual reports on BCMS improvement activities, such as management review, performance evaluation and corrective action

Enhancement processes, such as continual improvement, innovation and adaptation, drive changes in the BCMS. In order to implement these changes effectively, it is important that change management is incorporated into the continual improvement process. The change management process ensures that continual improvement is performed in an effective manner and provides a high degree of assurance that there are no undesired consequences as a result of the change.

It is useful to take into consideration the following points when implementing continual improvement:

- An appropriate risk assessment methodology should be adopted to evaluate proposed changes in the BCMS. The detail of assessment should be proportionate with the level of risk to the integrity of the BCMS.

- From the business continuity standpoint, the proposed improvement should help to strengthen the existing BCMS performance. It should be assessed against the requirements of the business continuity policy.

- Proposed improvement actions should be evaluated by the business continuity manager and approved by executive management. Once approved, they should be communicated to all who are involved in the continual improvement process. It is important to gain their support and that they understand their roles in contributing to the improvement of the BCMS.

- In the post-implementation, an assessment should be carried out to validate that the improvement actions have met the business continuity objectives and there is no deleterious impact on the BCMS performance.

Summary

The control system is a crucial process that ensures that performance deviation of the BCMS from its intended outcomes is minimized. It also ensures that management activities and staff actions conform to the stipulated requirements of the business continuity policy. In order to make incremental progress to the management effectiveness of the BCMS, the element of continual improvement should be embedded in the different stages of the management system lifecycle. This ensures that the BCMS remains effective in maintaining performance excellence in the organization's changing context.

CHECKLIST

This checklist is intended to support the business continuity management system (BCMS) development process	Yes	No	Action required
Does the organization have a clearly defined and approved BCM control system?	☐	☐	☐
Have the different types of nonconformities in the BCMS been identified and documented?	☐	☐	☐
Are appropriate remedial actions in place to eliminate nonconformities in the BCMS?	☐	☐	☐
Are follow-up actions in place to verify the adequacy of the adopted corrective actions?	☐	☐	☐
Does the organization's continual improvement programme cover all aspects of the BCMS, that is, the lifecycle of the management system?	☐	☐	☐

Further reading

Business Continuity Institute (2013) *Good Practice Guidelines: A guide to global good practice in business continuity*, Business Continuity Institute, Caversham

ISO 22301:2012 – Societal security – Business continuity management systems – Requirements

ISO 22313:2012 – Societal security – Business continuity management systems – Guidance

Conclusion

10

OVERVIEW

- This chapter first highlights the corporate motivation for adopting the BCMS and explains its application in the organization.
- Next, it discusses the management challenges of implementing the BCMS.
- Finally, the chapter offers a number of strategies to overcome the barriers of establishing an effective BCMS in the organization.

Application of BCMS

In the past few years many organizations, both public and private, have appreciated the value of adopting the BCMS in the delivery of their critical products and services. Like other management systems in the areas of quality, security, risk and environmental management, the BCMS is recognized as a systematic approach that enhances the management effectiveness of the BCM programme. The central tenet of the BCMS is its dynamic and flexible way of implementing business continuity based on the context of the organization. The BCMS establishes an appropriate business continuity capability to address the key issues that could impact the organization's ability to fulfil its objectives and obligations. To support the operating requirements of the BCMS, an evidence-based approach should be adopted. This comprises monitoring measures to identify nonconformities and controls to prevent further recurrence. In addition, the process of continual improvement is carried out to optimize the BCMS in order that its management processes remain effective and relevant to business.

These general concepts can be summed up in the four-stage paradigm of a typical ISO standard, that is, the Plan-Do-Check-Act cycle. Once a cycle has been completed, it will lead to another cycle of improvement. In essence, this is an ongoing, systematic approach to managing the BCMS performance. It is worth noting that ISO 22301 does not specify the required level of business continuity performance; rather it describes the elements that are essential to driving continual improvement in the BCMS.

In general, the corporate decision to adopt ISO 22301 is motivated by one or more of the following factors:

- Implement, maintain and improve the BCM programme
- Conform to good BCM practices
- Secure future opportunities, such as tenders and contracts
- Comply with the market norm of doing business
- Improve the organization's business continuity capability
- Underpin the organization's overall business performance

The costs and benefits of a BCMS will vary significantly depending on the time and resources management is willing to invest toward a full implementation of ISO 22301. This is naturally influenced by executive management's perception of the value that the BCMS adds to business. The most important resource invested in implementing the BCMS will be the time of staff. Generally, establishment of the BCMS will take time to become fully embedded as an integral part of mainstream management. Nonetheless, this investment of time will result in substantial benefits in the long term. Over time staff throughout the organization at all levels will become more conscious of how the BCMS optimizes product and service availability, as well as its role in supporting the business strategies. While some of the positive outcomes can be realized without implementing a full BCMS – through ad hoc or focused efforts, a formalized system approach provides a much greater chance of achieving benefits to business.

In general, the BCMS can be applied in the following areas:

- Corporate governance and leadership – The foundation of good governance is the ability to provide a sound system of internal controls to adequately manage the integrity of management activities. This is supported by the enterprise risk management (ERM) programme that monitors and controls these activities in order to minimize the undesired effects of risk on an organization's capital and earnings. Being an essential element of the ERM programme, the BCMS can be incorporated to strengthen management capability by establishing an effective response to minimize the impact of an incident on the organization. The management system also advocates that the senior leadership team act as the overall custodian of the BCMS. This enables the organization to comply with the necessary regulatory and legislative requirements.

- Critical product and service delivery – One of the key functions of the BCMS is to establish an adequate business continuity capability to safeguard the continuity of key products and services during an incident. It can be adopted to optimize resilience in critical workflows and support the effective utilization of organizational resources. In addition, it ensures that suppliers that contribute to the delivery of key products and services have adequate resilience to meet the organization's BCM requirements.

- Management system integration – It is a growing trend that organizations recognize the value of adopting multiple standards. Such an approach simplifies management systems, optimizes resources and establishes a common framework for continual improvement. ISO 22301, being a member of the family of ISO standards, comprises a set of principles and processes that are consistent with other disciplines, such as quality, security, risk and environmental management. Implementing ISO 22301 with another management system, like ISO 9001 (quality), helps to streamline processes and improve customer requirements, whilst ensuring the process of delivery is effectively safeguarded against potential threats of disruption.

Management challenges

Despite the potential benefits the BCMS brings to the organization, there are often organizational barriers to implementation. These barriers can take many forms and are often presented as management challenges. It is important to consider these issues when planning to implement the BCMS:

- Lack of executive commitment
- Lack of necessary knowledge, skills and experience
- Lack of financial support
- Lack of awareness

Lack of executive commitment

Gaining the full support of executive management is one of the key challenges in establishing a formal BCMS in the organization. In the absence of such high-level commitment, it is very likely that the BCMS will not succeed. One plausible reason for lack of support is that senior managers have not yet internalized the business needs of introducing a formal BCMS. Members of the management team may consider business continuity an important management activity but not yet recognize its ability to create business advantages by minimizing downtime and preserving shareholder value.

Lack of necessary knowledge, skills and experience

A lack of essential skills is a major barrier to implementing an effective BCMS. This could lead to a range of deficiencies in the BCMS, such as ill-defined business continuity objectives and policy or ineffective management of the BCM processes. This barrier is compounded by the fact that lack of knowledge will render the BCMS too complex and result in a lack of clarification on what exactly is required to establish an effective BCMS. In addition, limited experience with the BCMS can make it a difficult task to determine the appropriate actions to achieve its intended outcomes.

Lack of financial support

In most cases, a dedicated budget is required to implement and manage the BCMS. The budget has a direct impact on the resources invested to support the ongoing maintenance of the BCMS. It can also shape how ISO 22301 is adopted and implemented in the organization. Bear in mind that financial support is directly influenced by the executive commitment to business continuity.

Lack of awareness

The lack of awareness in business continuity can lead to misjudgement of the BCMS and its value in corporate planning. This can inhibit the creation of a positive culture to achieve its intended outcomes. In most cases, this is due to a lack of communication in promoting the importance of BCM and how it underpins business performance.

Table 10.1 offers a list of suggested strategies that can help to address the management challenges of implementing the BCMS. It is important to note that some activities are prerequisites to the implementation of a formal BCMS.

The following recommendations will support the strategies mentioned in Table 10.1:

- Before embarking on the BCMS, the organization should assess its motivation for adopting ISO 22301. It is useful to collate a body of evidence from other organizations or independent bodies to understand how ISO 22301 can help the organization to improve its business continuity capability.

- Prior to setting up the BCMS, it is imperative to gain the full support of executive management to ensure successful implementation of ISO 22301. The case for the BCMS should be supported by evidence of how it adds value to business. Executive management should be involved in the entire ISO 22301 lifecycle, that is, from the planning to improvement of the BCMS performance.

TABLE 10.1   Strategies for BCMS implementation

Management Challenges	Strategies
Lack of executive commitment	• Appoint a business continuity champion • Examine case studies of organizations in crisis • Align BCM to the organization's strategic direction and objectives • Relate BCM to corporate priorities • Use drivers such as corporate governance, compliance and stakeholder and regulatory requirements • Examine case studies of best practice organizations adopting the BCMS • Use evidence of non-compliance supported by corporate audits • Include BCM as an item in the agenda • Introduce high-level BCM awareness events and desktop exercises • Maximize the influence of the business continuity champion
Lack of necessary skills and other resources	• Seek external support • Seek professional certifications • Attend BCM courses • Recruit staff • Attend BCM events such as workshops, conferences and seminars • Mentor staff
Lack of financial resources	• Use staged implementation • Prioritize corporate projects • Negotiate budget • Integrate with other management systems • Incorporate into existing resilience activities

(Continued)

TABLE 10.1 (*Continued*)

Management Challenges	Strategies
Lack of communication	• Hold staff meetings • Roadshows by the BCM team • Use media such as posters, newsletters and a dedicated website to disseminate BCM information • Present on BCM topics • Convey messages from the business continuity champion or executive management
Lack of awareness	• Create a BCM awareness programme • Present on BCM topics • Emphasize benefits of BCM in the workplace • Develop simple messages to be assimilated into staff working practice • Introduce BCM awareness events and exercises • Deliver messages through electronic message boards, posters, bulletin boards, videos and personal communication to groups of staff

- For organizations with established risk and BCM programmes, it is useful to consider how ISO 22301 can build into the current processes and procedures.

- During the planning stage it is useful to gather feedback from across the organization, particularly from middle and operational management, which have good working knowledge on how ISO 22301 can be applied to critical activities.

- A series of business continuity presentations and awareness events can generate interest amongst staff. Such activities will help them to understand the importance of the BCMS and maximize the likelihood of embedding its concepts in corporate processes.

- For organizations that have experience in implementing other management systems, it can be effective to implement ISO 22301 by integrating BCM activities into existing management system processes to avoid duplicating efforts and resources.

- It is useful to seek advice from relevant stakeholders that might have experience with BCMS implementation. Their ideas can help to improve the implementation of the BCMS in the organization.

Concluding remarks

The enhanced status of BCM within organizations is evidenced by the launch of ISO 22301. Alongside quality, security, risk and environmental management, it is recognized as an important corporate activity. ISO 22301 is designed to provide guidance to organizations in the design and implementation of a management-owned and driven BCMS. It is a non-prescriptive framework that acknowledges there are many approaches to achieving an excellent BCMS in organizations, regardless of size, sector or BCM maturity. It gives the organization the flexibility to apply what is most relevant to its business and context. Whilst ISO 22301 is a recognized approach that encapsulates good BCM practices, it is not intended to develop the BCMS into a 'perfect' management process. Any attempt of that nature would defeat the spirit of the management system. Perhaps the most effective BCMS is one that continually adapts to stay relevant to the organization's long-term needs. Furthermore, no business continuity capability can remain effective without the knowledge and skills of staff who are responsible for managing the BCMS process, that is, the business continuity manager and members of the BCM team. Their level of competence will shape the way BCM is adopted and implemented in the organization. These individuals embody a diverse range of skills combined with knowledge acquired across management and technical disciplines. To ensure the BCMS can best adapt to a changing environment, the business continuity manager, and those with roles in the management system, will need to keep abreast of the latest developments in the BCM industry and be able to demonstrate that they have done so.

CHECKLIST

This checklist is intended to support the business continuity management system (BCMS) development process	Yes	No	Action required
Has the senior leadership team understood the benefits of implementing ISO 22301 – Business Continuity Management System?	☐	☐	☐
Have the barriers that impede the implementation of the BCMS been identified?	☐	☐	☐
Are there appropriate strategies and plans in place to maximize the success of implementing the BCMS in the organization?	☐	☐	☐

REFERENCES

Business Continuity Institute (2013) *Good Practice Guidelines: A guide to global good practice in business continuity*, Business Continuity Institute, Caversham

Bird, L (2011) *Dictionary of Business Continuity Management Terms*, Business Continuity Institute, Caversham

Disaster Recovery Institute International (DRII) (2012) *Professional Practices for Business Continuity Practitioners*, DRII, New York

Disaster Recovery Institute International (2013) *International Glossary for Resiliency*, DRII, New York

IEC 31010:2009 – Risk management – Risk assessment techniques

ISO 19011:2011 – Guidelines for auditing management systems

ISO 31000:2009 – Risk management – Principles and guidelines

ISO 22300:2012 – Societal security – Terminology

ISO 22301:2012 – Societal security – Business continuity management systems – Requirements

ISO 22313:2012 – Societal security – Business continuity management systems – Guidance

ISO 22320:2011 – Societal security – Emergency management – Requirements for incident response ISO 22398:2013 – Societal security – Guidelines for exercises

ISO Guide 73:2009 – Risk management – Vocabulary

ISO/IEC 17021:2011 – Conformity assessment – Requirements for bodies providing audit and certification of management systems

ISO/IEC 24762:2008 – Information technology – Security techniques – Guidelines for information and communications technology disaster recovery services

ISO/IEC 27001:2013 – Information technology – Security techniques – Information security management systems – Requirements

ISO/IEC 27002:2013 – Information technology – Security techniques – Code of practice for information security controls

ISO/IEC 27031:2011 – Information technology – Security techniques – Guidelines for information and communication technology readiness for business continuity

ISO/IEC 27036:2014 – Information technology – Security techniques – Information security for supplier relationships – Part 1: Overview and concepts

INDEX